THE BASICS

Body Studies: The Basics is an accessible introduction to the key concerns and debates surrounding the study of the sociological and physical body. Taking an interdisciplinary approach, it examines the body as a subject for study and discussing attitudes and debates surrounding new technologies, forms of modification, obesity, age and enfreakment being brought into focus by the media. It addresses such topics as:

- Nature vs. culture: how we "build" and transform our bodies
- Conformity and resistance in bodily practice
- Issues of body image – beauty, diet, exercise and age
- Sporting bodies and the pursuit of ideals
- Enfreakment, disability and monstrosity
- Cyborgs and virtual online bodies

With suggestions for further reading, a glossary of key terms and a range of historical and contemporary case studies, *Body Studies: The Basics* is essential reading for anyone studying the body in a cultural and sociological context.

Niall Richardson is Lecturer in Film, Media and Cultural Studies at the University of Sussex where he convenes the MA Gender and Media. He has written and edited numerous articles and books on issues of the body, including *Critical Readings in Bodybuilding* (2011) and *Transgressive Bodies: Representations in Film and Popular Culture* (2010).

Adam Locks is programme co-ordinator for Film and Television Studies and Media and Cultural Studies at University of Chichester. He is co-editor of the book *Critical Readings in Bodybuilding* (2011).

THE BASICS

BODY STUDIES

THE BASICS

Niall Richardson and Adam Locks

LONDON AND NEW YORK

First published 2014
by Routledge
2 Park Square, Milton Park, Abingdon, Oxon OX14 4RN

and by Routledge
711 Third Avenue, New York, NY 10017

Routledge is an imprint of the Taylor & Francis Group, an informa business

British Library Cataloguing in Publication Data
A catalogue record for this book is available from the British Library

Library of Congress Cataloging in Publication Data
Richardson, Niall.
Body studies : the basics / Niall Richardson and Adam Locks.
pages cm
1. Human body--Social aspects. I. Locks, Adam. II. Title.
HM636.R528 2014
301--dc23
2013044064

ISBN: 978-0-415-69619-7 (hbk)
ISBN: 978-0-415-69620-3 (pbk)
ISBN: 978-1-315-77715-3 (ebk)

Typeset in Bembo
by Taylor & Francis Books

Printed and bound in the United States of America by
Edwards Brothers Malloy on sustainably sourced paper

CONTENTS

PREFACE: I'VE GOT A BODY?

A very popular song for infants is 'The Body Song' and its first stanza is:

> I've got a body, a very busy body
> And it goes everywhere with me.
> And on that body I've got a nose
> And it goes everywhere with me.
> And I sniff sniff here, sniff sniff there,
> Sniff, sniff, sniff, sniff everywhere.
> I've got a body, a very busy body
> And it goes everywhere with me.

The song then goes on to cite all the various body parts that a person has and suggests appropriate movements that the person could make with these body parts. For example, the singer of the song can clap their hands and stamp their feet at the relevant sections. The song concludes with the proclamation that it's good to have a body because 'my body is me'.

Although this little song is designed to encourage physical coordination in very young children (especially movement in time to music), it also summarises two of the key themes that are important in the critical study of the body. Namely, people have bodies (very busy bodies) but they also *are* their bodies. Indeed, these are two of the key issues that we will be exploring in the chapters of this book.

First, the body is the way in which we make sense of the world and our environments. In this sense the body is, as the song describes, very busy as it is always engaging with our surroundings. We experience life through our bodies and our senses of touch, smell, sight, sound and taste allow us to interpret the world around us. Humans are always located in some particular place, and at some particular time, and our awareness is profoundly influenced by the fact that we have a body. This concept is known as embodiment and ideas about embodiment are relevant to many fields, including religion, science, medicine and philosophy. One of the areas of critical thought which has considered the issue of embodiment in considerable detail is phenomenology. Phenomenology literally translates into the "study of phenomena" and is a philosophy, or method of inquiry, based on the premise that reality consists of objects and events *as they are perceived or understood in human consciousness* and not of anything independent of human consciousness. Again, to stress the point, we perceive or understand objects and events through our bodies. Therefore, philosophers have argued (Merleau-Ponty 1976, 1981) that the world comes to us *via perceptive awareness* – i.e. the place of our body in the world. We come to understand our relation to the world via the positioning of our bodies.

However, the body is not merely an object in the world (we do not only *have* "busy" bodies) but we also *are* our bodies in that the body is the vehicle for our expression in the world. Indeed, the body can be read as '*the visible form of our intentions*' (Merleau-Ponty 1976: 5). The body is the site for the articulation of all our identifications of gender, class, sexuality, race, ethnicity and religion. As the following chapters of this book will argue, we are all of us body-builders as we all build and style our bodies on a daily basis (see chapter 1). We decide how we want to dress and style our bodies; we decide how much hair we want on our bodies and we shave, wax and even have IPL or electrolysis to remove hair permanently; we manipulate our bodies' weight through diet and exercise and we may even modify our bodies to extreme levels (see chapter 5) and introduce mechanical agents into our bodies merging flesh and technology (see chapter 6).

However, the key argument of this book is that although the body may well be the way of expressing our intentions, there are limitations placed upon us all as to how we "wear" and "use" our bodies. Underpinning the subsequent chapters is the argument that the body is enthralled to cultural regimes (Foucault 1977: 25) and that, at any time, we are subject to discourses telling us how we should look – especially how we should dress and what our bodies' weight (fat levels) should be. In our hypermediated society we are constantly assailed with media images – especially advertisements representing "appropriate" bodies – so that we internalise these "ideals" and either attempt to conform to them or resist them (see chapters 1 and 2). In this respect, the body is enthralled to specific cultural discourses of gender, sexuality and class and we constantly worry about whether our bodies match up to these ideals. On a daily basis, a woman may wonder: Am I dressed in a fashion that is "suitably" feminine? Not too overtly "sexual"? Not too "cheap"? Of course, as these examples show there is considerably more pressure on the female body to conform to expectations. As chapter 1 will explain, there has always been a tradition of women being identi-fied simply *as* their bodies. While masculinity has more often been associated with the intellect and reason, femininity is appraised in terms of its physical beauty.

Yet although the body is enthralled to the regimes of specific cultures, it is important to remember that not all cultures have the same requirements. For example, there is a very different requirement of dress for the university student than there is for the banker. While jeans and T-shirts may well be acceptable in the university seminar room, such iconography would be very unacceptable in the city bank. Nevertheless, there is always the potential for resistance (see chapter 2) and it is fair to say that whenever resistance first appears it is always expressed through the body. Therefore, bodies only make sense – are interpretable – within specific cultures and periods. For example, a body that carries a little extra adipose tissue may, nowadays, be identified as "fat" and "unattractive" while in earlier periods (especially times when there wasn't enough food) to be plump would have been read as healthy and therefore very attractive. In other words, bodies only make sense within specific cultural contexts.

This short, introductory textbook attempts to address these two issues throughout all its chapters. People do indeed have bodies, and these bodies provide an understanding of what it means to exist in the world, but people also *are* their bodies and the iconography of our bodies is our means of expression, our articulation of identification. It could be argued that we live at a time when there has never been so much focus upon not only our own body, but also upon the bodies of others who do not match up to ideas of what is deemed acceptable (see chapter 4). Images in the media often make us worry about our own appearance and the media has often been accused of generating self-hatred and body fascism (chapter 3). The following chapters will consider in more detail how much expression and what type of identification "may" be articulated through the body and analyse the importance of body image in contemporary culture in considerably more detail.

The children's chorus 'The Body Song' is correct to assert that we all have bodies – very busy bodies – but in our contemporary culture of media imagery and body fascism are any of us happy to sing the final line and proclaim with pride that the 'body is me'?

BODY
NATURE OR CULTURE?

It seems that contemporary culture is obsessed with the body. We only have to turn on the television any night of the week to find programmes dedicated to the body, especially its performance and appearance. At any moment, we are likely to be told, from a variety of media, how the body *should* act and *should* look. We have programmes telling us how we *should* dress, what our weight *should* be, how we *should* spend our leisure time and even how our bodies *should* age. Indeed, make-over shows – once a segment tagged onto morning chat shows – have now become prime time entertainment (see Palmer 2008). Yet, while contemporary culture seems to evidence an obsession with regimenting bodies into "appropriate" performances, popular entertainment has also demonstrated a resurging fascination with bodies that do not conform to expectations; bodies that, for whatever reason, are deemed to be "freakish" and outside the norm. Indeed, a number of these shows, although often couched within medical discourses, can be identified as little more than revised versions of the archaic "freak" show (see Gamson 1998; Richardson 2010).

Arguably, one of the reasons for the increasing fascination with the body is an acknowledgement that the body is not fixed or essential but (to a certain extent) flexible. We are all involved, to varying degrees, in what Chris Shilling has termed 'body projects'

(2003). The body may be biological (it is undoubtedly flesh and blood) but it is also cultural in that we all shape and manipulate our bodies. As we tell our students, we are all of us body-builders in that we are all involved in building and styling our bodies on a daily basis. We all diet in order to control the weight of our bodies, either by engaging in a specific dietary regime or simply by watching our calories after a time of indulgence; we all engage in some form of exercise, whether it is to build muscle, lose fat or simply to shape and tone the body; we change or manipulate our skin tone through (fake) tanning or application of make-up; we manipulate our hair – both on our heads and on our bodies – when we cut, shave, wax or preen; we select clothes which style and reshape our bodies and many of us engage in more invasive cosmetic procedures which can range from orthodontic realignment of the teeth through to cosmetic surgery. In short, contemporary culture views the body as a life-long project which requires dedication, work and effort.

In this respect, we no longer think of the body as an essentialist attribute but in terms of socio-cultural constructionism. While essentialism views identity as something fixed and immutable, constructionism argues that identity should be entitled "identification" in that it changes according to culture, era and context (see Hall 1992). For example, a body that is deemed "fat" in one particular context or culture may not be deemed so in another. In times of hardship, when there was not enough food, carrying more adipose tissue on the body was desirable and a signifier of affluence. Now, in contemporary Western culture's time of fast-food abundance, it is more desirable to be thinner. This identification can then be further problematised when we start considering subcultural identifications within contemporary culture. For example, a body which is deemed "average" weight in the university classroom may be deemed "overweight" if it were placed in the context of, say, a ballet class or a gymnastics session. In other words, the signification of the body – and its subsequent identification – depends upon the particular culture and context in which that body is located.

This example of weight identification, however, stresses an important point: the body is "political" as its iconography (appearance) signifies conformity or resistance to contemporary cultural requirements. As Michel Foucault famously argued, 'The body is directly involved in a political field; power relations have an immediate hold upon it: they invest it, mark it, train it, torture it, force it to carry out tasks, to perform ceremonies, to emit signs' (1977: 25). In this respect, the body is always implicated in a dialogue with cultural discourses – conforming to, resisting and negotiating the requirements of the culture.

For example, the 1920s saw the iconography of the flapper enter into Western culture. Flappers were young, "modern" women who were attempting to articulate their emancipation by styling their bodies in a different fashion from previous generations. Women were now cutting their hair into bobs; wearing short, pageboy-type smock dresses, which revealed ankles and calves; and often strapping down their breasts to attain a flatter cleavage. Obviously this particular look was demonstrating a number of negotiations with cultural and political discourses. On one level it was signifying a form of female liberation and was articulating feminine sexuality – especially through the revelation of the lower leg. Given that, in previous generations, exposure of the limbs would have been deemed *obscene* this was a very definite reaction to earlier, more oppressive times. Yet the flapper's iconography also downplayed other elements of feminine sexuality, which had been acceptable displays in earlier times, by covering the shoulders, downplaying any attention to the cleavage and rejecting cinched waists and hourglass figures through wearing the smock dresses. In other words, the flapper's iconography signifies a negotiation taking place in which women were debating ideas of sexuality, liberation and empowerment through a performance of the body. Indeed, whenever resistance takes places it nearly always starts with some sort of negotiation of the body's iconography (see chapter 2).

However, as the example of the flapper illustrates, the body is only interpretable within a specific culture and context. If a young woman in contemporary Western culture were to adopt the look of the flapper it would not – could not – signify in the same way as it did in 1920s culture. Therefore, while Foucault argued that the body was 'directly involved in a political field', it was Judith Butler who developed these debates in more recent years by arguing that the body only has significance within a specific culture or context (1990, 1993). There cannot be an interpretable body without the cultural regimes which both inscribe but also give it a particular meaning or reify it. Butler famously asked 'is there a "physical" body prior to the perpetually perceived body? An *impossible* question to decide' (1990, my emphasis). What Butler's question is asking is whether a body *can* have any signification outside of a specific context or cultural regime. In other words, the body is formed through an engagement with specific cultural regimes and so outside of this particular context the body cannot make sense or be interpretable. For example, if we consider professional, competitive-level *extreme* bodybuilding culture we will find a group of bodies who, through a process of diet, exercise and (possible/probable) hormonal manipulation, have built the voluntary muscles of their bodies to *huge* dimensions and dieted to remove subcutaneous fat to enhance vascularity (the "bulging veins" look of bodybuilding culture). Many people who are located outside of the subculture of bodybuilding find such extreme bodies to be odd, strange or even disgusting. People may question why someone would want to look like that. They may think that such an extreme body has difficulty fitting into the confines of public transport, let alone fashionable clothes, so why would someone want to do that to him/herself? Yet, within the context of bodybuilding culture, these bodies are exalted and viewed as "ideal". For those involved in the (sub)culture of bodybuilding, the professional bodybuilder's physique signifies supreme dedication to the sport, an absolute mind-over-matter control and unparalleled "beauty". In other words, the meaning of the body – the signification of the body – only makes sense within a specific culture in which participants are aware of the discourses and the requirements of the culture. To the person outside of bodybuilding (sub)culture those bodies are un-interpretable and do not make sense. To someone immersed in bodybuilding culture, the bodies' specific politics can be understood. In order for the body to make sense, or be readable, it must be immersed within the specific politics of a culture. After all, if somebody was living in desert island isolation how would that person know if he/she was tall or short, fat or thin, good looking or plain? We only gain a sense of self, a sense of identification, through interaction with culture. Our bodies, their specific signification, only make sense through cultural regimes and so we are continuously negotiating those cultural requirements through our bodies' performances and iconography. At a very simple level, this may even be following a particular fashion trend in clothes or hairstyle or it may be a requirement to attain a specific weight through diet and exercise or a specific feature through more invasive surgical procedures (see chapter 3).

However, despite the fact that there is an awareness of the (relative) plasticity or flexibility of the body, contemporary culture seems to maintain a narrow prescription about "appropriate" iconography. Most "make-over narratives" – whether fiction film texts or actual make-over shows – reinforce hegemonic ideas of masculinity and femininity (see Richardson and Wearing 2014). Indeed, most make-over narratives attempt to revise a body that is failing to perform "appropriate" femininity and reshape that body so that it accords with received ideas. If a body refuses to perform "appropriate" iconography then it is often subject to enfreakment strategies and represented as a figure of ridicule, a "freak" (see chapter 4).

THE CARTESIAN DUALISM

One important theory, that has been very influential in our consideration of the body, has been the "Cartesian Dualism". Inspired by the writings of the philosopher René Descartes (trans. 1969), the "Cartesian Dualism" argues that there has always been a distinction maintained between the head/mind and the body. While the head is the source of the intellect and of reason, the body has always been associated with unruly emotion and excess and this key dichotomy has been deployed in all discourses from medicine, law and religion through to literary and artistic representations. Any activity which is deemed to be worthwhile is an enlightenment of the intellect or mind. Even sporting activities, although celebrating the accomplishments of the body, praise the mind's control for having disciplined the body rather than the power of the body itself. This dichotomy is played out across all discourses from medicine through to religions. In Christianity, for example, devotional art often represents saints or martyrs who are being tortured and crucified. Yet while the saint's body may be wracked with pain, the head is usually elevated to heaven, and lit beatifically, thus suggesting how the mind has transcended the body and moved beyond its vulgar, base confines.

Susan Bordo – arguably the "godmother" of Body Studies – explains how the tradition of this dualist axis (the mind/body split) can be traced back to classical philosophy (1993: 144–146). First, there is the tradition that the body is not the "self" or the actual person but simply the shell or the outer casing for the true being. Whether we credit the Christian tradition of the soul, or simply ascribe to the idea of the intellect as the true self, we do not view the outer casing or shell as the actual person. Second, this outer casing of the body is often viewed as a confinement or even a limitation. Again, this is certainly the teachings of Christianity but also a philosophy shared by anyone who has often found that his/ her body has been a hindrance – too tired, too weak, too fragile – and an impediment to success. Third, and following this idea, the body is viewed as the enemy. How often do we feel that if only the body were not subject to tiredness, hunger and pain we would be able to make greater progress in our chosen activity? Bordo quotes Plato who writes that the body is:

> a source of countless distractions by reason of the mere requirement of food. It is liable also to diseases which overtake and impede us in the pursuit of truth; it fills us full of loves, and lusts, and fears, and fancies of all kinds, and endless foolery, and in very truth, as men say, takes away from us the power of thinking at all. Whence come wars, and fightings, and factions? Whence but from the body and the lusts of the body?
>
> (1993: 145)

Fourth, as Plato argues above, there is the important idea that the body must be suppressed and disciplined. Given that all "bad" things happen in the world because of the "unruly" body, civilization must control the bodily urges and discipline them, subject them to the discipline of the mind. To be human – in other words, to be more than animal – the mind must control and subjugate the body. Indeed, this underpins all the "civilized" rituals that culture has celebrated, ranging from training for sports, to Christian fasting rituals to scholarship in the arts and sciences. People who are reviled and criticised are the people who are thought to have failed to attain the mind/body hierarchy and have allowed the body to overwhelm the intellect. A person who is overweight, for example, is criticised for having no discipline over his/her body and is thought to be just like animals who eat whatever they want, whenever they want. School children who refuse to practise their musical instrument or attend sport classes are criticised for having no self-discipline, and parents worry that their child will not do well in life as he/she does not demonstrate the necessary mind over matter that is required to "succeed" in society.

However, this dualist axis of mind over matter is also mapped onto other socio-cultural identifications of class, race and – the most important one – gender (see Bordo 1993). First, the mind/body split is classed. The upper echelons of society – especially the respected professions such as medicine, Church, education – are associated with the intellect. Again, although professional sports men and women are praised for their accomplishments of the body, it is their mental discipline – their control of the body – that is celebrated and prized. By contrast, the lower echelons such as peasants, labourers and manual workers are thought of only in terms of their bodies. Factory work, arguably, requires little intellect, merely repetitive manual work.

Second, the dualist axis is also raced. There is a history of representing non-white bodies simply *as* their bodies. Popular culture yields a tradition of offensive stereotypes of how African-American bodies are more animal-like or savage than their white counterparts. Hollywood cinema, for example, had a tradition of representing black slaves as uncontrolled and undisciplined by ignoring the history of why the slaves' bodies behaved in the way they did. One of Hollywood's cruellest racial stereotypes was the Mammy. Mammy was a black, female slave (often on a cotton plantation) who served as a nanny/nursemaid to the owners' children. Hollywood often represented Mammy as a source of humour because she was extremely fat but the representations always concealed the actual history of why the Mammy was so big. Mammy, as a slave on the cotton plantation, would often have been *used* as a "baby-making machine", producing more slaves for the plantation. After innumerable subsequent pregnancies, Mammy would have lost her figure and now, worn out with so many pregnancies, would have been no use in the cotton field and so was put to work in the household as a nursemaid of the children. Representations in popular culture, however, do not reveal the details of the history but simply focus on the Mammy's sheer physical size, suggesting that she has been unable to control her body's appetite and hence become so fat. Like all stereotypes, the representation of Mammy encouraged spectators to laugh at the consequence without any awareness of the cause. Similarly, representing black slaves who had a *humorous* walk was standard fare in Hollywood. Slaves were often represented with an uncoordinated shuffle or hobble thus suggesting that they could not control their bodies and so warranted no better position in society. However, this stereotype again disguised the fact that this hobbling walk was probably as a result of the plantation owner cutting the slaves' Achilles' tendon in order to prevent the slaves from running away. Both the "fat Mammy" and the "hobbling slave" created an impression of black bodies being uncoordinated, uncivilized and, most importantly, unable to discipline their bodies. They were not bodies controlled by the mind; they simply were their bodies. Although these stereotypes are no longer permitted in popular culture, more "positive" representations of black bodies still reinforce the connection of body and race. For example, the stereotype of black bodies being innately or inherently rhythmical (they just feel the beat of the music and dance so much better than their white neighbours) may, on one level, be deemed complimentary but it also reinforces the idea of black bodies as being more physical and therefore less cerebral or civilized than their white counterparts.

Finally, the dualist axis is gendered. There has always been a tradition of women simply being their bodies. As Elizabeth Spelman famously argued:

> Woman has been portrayed as essentially a bodily being, and this image has been used to deny her full status as a human being wherever and whenever mental activity as over against bodily activity has been thought to be the most human activity of all.
>
> (1982: 123)

While men have always been associated with reason, intellect and scholarship (the "great" minds of civilization have always been *assumed* to be men), women have always been identified in terms of their bodies. For example, the female body is thought to be "held" by the lunar cycle and menstruates according to the specific "time of the month". In other words, women are enthralled to nature while men move beyond the confines of nature to succeed to the realms of culture. For example, this highly offensive dismissal of women as simply being enthralled to their bodies can be seen in the way in which bad temper is still so often interpreted according to gender. If a man is irritable then something is upsetting or annoying him. If a woman is irritable, people (i.e. men) often assume that it's her "time of the month". This conflation of woman as body continues in the association of women with all bodily activities such as pregnancy, birth and breast feeding. Indeed, in horror cinema when bodies become monstrous, through being excessive, out of control and undisciplined, they are usually feminised (see Creed 1992) and assume the activities associated with femininity – especially those related to birth and menstruation. In horror cinema, bodies swell, gestate, leak and often expel an alien life form which is growing inside. Although horror cinema offers extreme examples, the other end of the cultural hierarchy – fine art – has always represented women simply as their bodies. The tradition of the female nude (see Nead 1992) has always portrayed women as valued only because of their bodies and indeed the motif of representing a female nude gazing upon her own reflection in a mirror is an invitation to the spectator to objectify, without guilt, the body on display (see Berger 1975). If the female nude enjoys gazing upon her own reflection, in auto-erotic delight, then the (male) spectator should not feel any anxiety. By contrast, the representation of the male body in art is always a testament to the power and authority of that body rather than its physical beauty. We gaze in awe at Hercules slaying the Hydra and marvel at the strength of his body rather than its beauty (see Berger 1975).

Often this tradition of equating women with their bodies is essentialised by culture even though it is simply a cultural construct. There was a long tradition, supported by many "actual" cases, of women being identified as the "delicate sex", often given to swooning or passing out. Pseudo medical science essentialised this by blaming the woman's womb (a biological element of her body) for this behaviour and coined the term "hysteria" – which translates into "wandering womb" (*hysteron* is the Greek for womb). The medical "cure" for this condition was the smelling salts whose vile vapours would drive the womb back down where it was supposed to be. Of course, although women were indeed actually swooning and fainting, it had nothing to do with loose internal organs but with the tradition of corsetry in which a woman was laced up so tightly in her whalebone corset that she could barely breathe. This example of hysteria/swooning shows how culture identified women simply *as* their bodies, and excused this behaviour as an essential or fixed aspect of femininity, when in fact it was a cultural construct engineered through the tradition of corsetry.

In this respect, gender is an important area of discussion within contemporary Body Studies. Until relatively recently, men had the luxury of not having to consider themselves as gendered and they certainly did not have to think of their identification in terms of the body's appearance. Indeed, men who *were* too invested in their appearance may well have been regarded with suspicion and identified as gay or else even "imbalanced". Although this has certainly changed and men (both gay and straight) are feeling the tyranny of body image, women are still, despite the advancements of feminist politics, considered in terms of their body's appearance (see chapter 3). Indeed, one particularly insidious cultural shift in contemporary gender politics has been contemporary culture's attempt to reconcile feminine iconography with feminism. According to media discourses, the contemporary postfeminist can be feminist while performing extreme girlishness. Although some do see this as a laudable area of postfeminism most critics are more sceptical and see this as a form of backlash in which the achievements of feminism have been negated (see Douglas 2010; McRobbie 1997, 2009; Gill 2007; Walter 2010). Young women are being told that it is empowering to be objectified. Is this because we now live in an equal society or is it a backlash against feminist politics, returning us to a prefeminist era?

BODY STUDIES

This book is intended as an introduction to the popular area of scholarship now known as Body Studies. It does not claim to offer an in-depth consideration of all the relevant debates and issues but merely to *introduce* students to this fascinating area of scholarship. As such, it is intended for the undergraduate or the student who is encountering these debates for the first time. Although we are addressing complex issues, we have tried to keep the writing as accessible as possible and to make the text as lively and entertaining as we can.

Chapter 2 will develop the issues already raised in this chapter by considering issues of conformity and resistance. Drawing upon a

Foucauldian framework, the chapter will consider how the body is implicated in discourses of power and how these are inflected by issues of gender, class and race. It will consider the Foucauldian thesis which argues that the body is instrumental in regimes of power and discipline and consider how this can be seen to work through contemporary culture's obsession with body image and make-over narratives. However, the chapter will also consider the possibility of resistance. Whenever resistance to cultural regimes starts it is nearly always manifested in the body, and so the chapter will consider the potential for resistance and consider bodies which challenge the idea of the norm and how transgressive displays may have the potential of challenging regimes and forcing a reconsideration of what is deemed normative and acceptable.

Chapter 3 will consider the multibillion pound business of the beauty industry. In the last few years there has been a dramatic increase in concerns with beautification. As Naomi Wolf has argued, beauty is now sold as the central concern and focus for women and, drawing upon the debates raised in chapter 2, this focus on beauty may be read as an attempt to configure women as docile bodies. On the other hand, other critics have argued that women have far more agency in their consumption of idealised images of beauty. This chapter examples the multitude of messages that abound around thinness, beauty and dieting and the way that they suggest the female body as some-*thing* that must always be perfected. The chapter then addresses ageing – a timely topic in contemporary Body Studies. Arguably, its popularity lies in the fact that "growing old" is something which *directly* affects everyone, unlike other identifications such as, say, ethnicity or disability. Provided we stick around long enough, we will all experience "old" age. Like all identifications, ageing is not merely biological but cultural. Bodies will age biologically but how this is *identified* is culturally mutable and inflected by factors such as gender, sexuality, race and class.

Chapter 4 considers the other side of the coin from contemporary culture's "beauty-ism": enfreakment. While a great deal of popular culture is devoted to the regulation of the body, the policing of the body into an "appropriate" image through make-over shows and advertising, the other side of popular culture has been a resurgence in the archaic spectacle of the "freak" show (see Richardson 2010). A considerable amount of media is given over to representations which delight in extreme bodies – bodies which do not conform to the canon of the ideal. This chapter will review the history of the "freak" show and the ambivalent response which it evoked in its spectators. Was the "freak" show an exploitation of disadvantaged bodies – bodies which we would now term disabled – or was it a spectacle which forced the spectator to question the very idea of the normative? In addressing these issues, the chapter will outline the cultural paradigms of disability studies and how the social model replaced the early medical model. This chapter then progresses to explaining the principles of "enfreakment" – a term first coined by David Hevey and developed by academic critics such as Garland Thomson (1996), Bogdan (1988) and Richardson (2010). Enfreakment argues that the body may well be unusual or even strange but that it is the strategy of representation which renders this different body a "freak". As such, "freak" is always a misrepresentation (see Bogdan 1988). The chapter will explore the politics of enfreakment imagery in contemporary popular culture and will conclude with an analysis of some contemporary "freak" shows in popular culture – ranging from television programmes such as *Embarrassing Bodies* to the cultural practice of extreme, competitive bodybuilding.

Chapter 5 considers how the body may be modified through practices such as tattooing, scarification, piercing or (extreme) bodybuilding. As this chapter will explain, we are all body-builders in that we are all engaged in various body projects, building our bodies in order to conform to hegemonic standards. However, there are also bodies which actively resist cultural hegemony and modify body image as an act of rebellion. This chapter will explore these acts of resistance in more detail and consider the potential of the act of transgression. How transgressive is transgressive? Although the transgressor is crossing one boundary he is, arguably, positioning him/herself within another (sub)culture in which the regulations of body image are even more restrictive than hegemonic culture. This chapter will consider the politics of acts such as tattooing, scarification and extreme bodybuilding as practices which evoke a self-reflexive acknowledgement of the body as a cultural project.

Finally, chapter 6 considers debates around cyborgs which are increasingly relevant for Body Studies as the interface between human and machine becomes intensified. The cyborg is a category that blurs the distinction between human and non-human. In film and literature, representations of the cyborg have traditionally focused on the classical cyborg, namely a human who has replaceable body parts. But more recent depictions have explored the post-classical cyborg where the body is left behind through downloading one's consciousness into cyberspace or an artificial body. Another version of the two is mind implants that would allow a cyborg either to download other people's experiences into their own mind (so that someone with the body of a white male heterosexual could experience what it would be like to be an Asian female and gay). Or, rather than retaining the body the person started with, he/she could transfer consciousness to another cyborg body. The chapter has several aims. First, to make clear the differences between the categories of robot, android and cyborg which are often muddled and confused. Second, to discuss the utopian and dystopian representations of the cyborg in media representations and in actual cyberspace (through Facebook, Second Life, etc.). Finally, to examine cyborgs in relation to body modification practices and, in this case, develop the debates already raised in chapter 5.

As we've stated already, this textbook is intended as a *basic* introduction to these debates. It does not promise all the "answers" and, given its word length, can really only hope to initiate scholarship in this area for the novice student. In all of the chapters, we will be referencing key critics/theorists in the relevant debates and we should hope that the student can then progress to engaging with the primary writing on these topics. One of the difficulties, for the novice student, is that a great of deal of writing within Body Studies can seem daunting and inaccessible. There is nothing more disheartening for an academic than to find his/her students shrugging shoulders and declaring that this week's reading task was "too difficult". We hope that this book will help to address these issues. The chapters aim to provide basic introductions to the debates and therefore equip the student for tackling the primary material. At the end of the book we have included a glossary which summarises/explains some of the key terms used in the chapters.

Finally, we should say that this area of scholarship is (in our opinion) one of the most fascinating and exciting areas within contemporary academia. Whether we work in film studies, cultural studies, media studies, sociology, sports studies, visual culture, art history or gender studies, we cannot help but be intrigued by the debates about the body and embodiment. Body Studies can *never* be abstract debates. By the very fact of having a body we are all implicated in these discourses. Whether we are subject to the tyranny of body image, making our personal stand of resistance via body modification or simply in awe of the political importance of the body within contemporary regimes, we hope that this book will hold some relevance for the reader and inspire any student to continue further scholarship in these debates.

RECOMMENDED READING

Bordo, Susan (1993) *Unbearable Weight: Feminism, Western Culture, and the Body* (Berkeley, CA: University of California Press)

Arguably, Bordo can be termed the "godmother" of Body Studies and this text is viewed by many as one of the first in this area of scholarship. Drawing upon a Foucauldian framework, *Unbearable Weight* has inspired innumerable scholars largely because it was one of the first to demonstrate the importance of critical and cultural theory for the lived experience of the gendered self. *Beautifully* written and drawing upon relevant cultural examples, Bordo's text is essential reading for anyone hoping to engage with Body Studies.

Richardson, Niall (2010) *Transgressive Bodies: Representations in Film and Popular Culture* (Farnham: Ashgate)

Although this book is intended as an examination of how strategies of enfreakment continue in a variety of contemporary media, *Transgressive Bodies* introduces the reader to constructionist debates of the body and contains short introductions to each section which summarise the critical writing on a variety of different bodies.

Shildrick, Margrit and Price, Janet (eds) (1999) *Feminist Theory and the Body: A Reader* (Edinburgh: Edinburgh University Press)

An extremely important edited collection which was, arguably, the first to collect feminist writings about the body. This book is edited by internationally recognised scholars of the body and the material has been beautifully organised so as to guide the student through the progressions and developments of the arguments.

Shilling, Chris (2003) *The Body and Social Theory* (London: Sage)

This much reprinted text remains one of the key introductions to Body Studies within a sociological framework. Shilling reviews the existing literature in considerable detail and makes some very complex theories accessible to the student.

CONFORMITY OR RESISTANCE?

In the previous chapter, we cited Michel Foucault who argued that 'the body is directly involved in a political field' (1977: 25). Power relations work through and on the body by demanding "appropriate" performance and iconography. Yet while culture may demand conformity to particular discourses, there is always the potential for resistance and when resistance starts it nearly always commences with the body. This chapter attempts to introduce the key debates within a consideration of conformity and resistance and the place of the body within these dynamics.

In early European culture (periods we now refer to as the Dark Ages) physical torture was a common form of punishment and a means of controlling and disciplining people. Such was the popularity of torture that there were professional torturers employed to invent new and horrific means of inflicting unbearable sensations on the victims' bodies. The point of torture was to wreak excruciating pain in the subject's body while still keeping that person alive. Often a variety of tortures would take place in seclusion, an indoor torture chamber, in which bodies would be subjected to horrors such as being stretched on the rack or pressed under enormous weight. However, a great deal of torture would occur in a public place as a spectacle for all the other citizens of the town or village. For example, for moderate crimes, bodies could be publically flogged and there were various instruments available to inflict the utmost pain. (The "cat-o'-nine-tails" was a specialised whip which divided into nine switches in order to exact the greatest amount of pain with each lash. This instrument of torture has given us the sayings "let the cat out of the bag" and "no room to swing a cat".) Alternatively, bodies could be placed in the stocks for a period of time thus causing the body to become contorted and wracked with pain or the particular torture could punish a specific part of the body that was deemed appropriate to the crime. For example, a pickpocket may have fingers severed from the hand in a public spectacle.

The intention of public torture was to achieve a number of things. First, public torture was supposed to make the guilty person the herald of his/her own condemnation. Torture was a public spectacle in which the accused would be charged and should admit his/her guilt. Second, torture often pinned the torture onto the crime itself. Torture spectacles were often carried out at the very place where the crime had been committed and, as we've already pointed out, may well have punished a specific part of the body that was involved in the crime. Third, torture reinforced the importance of the Christian tradition of confession. The guilty should confess their crime, suffer their penance and then be deemed no longer guilty. They would have paid/atoned for their guilt. Finally, and related to the last point, torture anticipated the punishments of the "after life" – the torments of hell – and the damnations of hell were very popular teachings within established Christianity at the time. Of course, underpinning all of these was an attempt to discipline and control the population of the specific place. Public torture was about instructing the citizen that his/her body was under the control of the Church and State and not a person's own private property. Torture was supposed to instil in the people an awareness of public discipline: how they were controlled by the legal, societal and cultural powers of the time.

However, it eventually became apparent that public torture was not attaining its goals. Public torture was supposed to represent the guilty person as a "monster" ("behold this evil pickpocket!") but the spectacle often evoked the very opposite and made the guilty person appear sympathetic – a victim of cruel punishments. Most importantly, torture failed to address the key principle that underpins most "civilised" traditions (which we discussed in chapter 1): the Cartesian Dualism. Torture may well be assailing and punishing the body, but it was doing little to challenge or punish the mind. The shoplifter's hand was not the guilty element; it was his/her mind. Severing the person's hand would not stop subsequent shoplifting unless the criminal's mind could be changed.

For this reason, torture was abolished as a mechanism of punishment and public control. However, as various critics have argued, a "trace" of torture still remains and in contemporary culture this is most evident in film/media, especially contemporary horror films in which the spectacle of bodies being punished and tortured is popular entertainment for a certain type of spectator. Various critics have even labelled a subgenre of horror film "torture porn" in that the films' narratives seem to be structured around pornographied scenes of gratuitous torture.

When torture was abolished it was replaced by imprisonment as the sanctioned form of discipline. Bodies were no longer controlled and disciplined through physical intervention but by suspending their human rights and liberties. As Foucault argued, 'From being an art of unbearable sensations, punishment has become an economy of suspended rights' (1977: 11). The Church and State no longer invade the body to inflict unbearable pain upon it but imprison it in order to 'deprive the individual of a liberty that is regarded as a right and as a property' (11). Therefore, imprisonment replaced torture as the means of discipline and the *ideal* prison was designed by Jeremy Bentham and is called the panopticon.

A panopticon is an amphitheatre of prison cells, surrounding a central warden's tower. The architecture of this prison provides an ideal method for surveillance as all the prison cells in the periphery are under the constant gaze of the warden in the tower. Prisoners soon learn that their every move is under the scrutiny of the prison warden and they cannot do anything in their cells without being watched. Eventually, the prison inmates become so aware of the constant surveillance that they internalise this gaze and become self-policing subjects. After a period of time, it doesn't even matter if there actually is a warden in the tower surveying the cells as each prisoner will have adopted the regime of self-discipline. As Foucault explains, this is the ideal means of disciplining bodies and is much more efficient than physical torture or violence. 'There is no need for arms, physical violence, material constraints. Just a gaze. An inspecting gaze, a gaze which each individual under its weight will end by *interiorizing* to the point that he is his own overseer, each individual thus exercising this surveillance over, and against himself (1977: 155).

Thus the panopticon's system of self-surveillance is the perfect metaphor for how power functions in society. As Nancy Fraser summarises:

> Modern power ... is more penetrating than earlier forms of power. It gets hold of its subject at the deepest level, in their gestures, bodies and desires ... . Moreover modern power, as first developed in disciplinary micropractices, is not essentially situated in some central institutions (such as king, sovereign, ruling class, state, army etc.) rather, it is everywhere. As the description of the panoptical self surveillance demonstrated, it is even in the target themselves, in their bodies, gestures, desires and habits. In other words, as Foucault often says, modern power is capillary. It does not emanate from some central source, but circulates throughout the entire social body down even to the tiniest and apparently more trivial extremities.
>
> (1989: 24)

As Fraser argues, power is not "wielded" by a ruler but works in a more subtle way through subjects internalising the rules or discourses of a particular culture and accepting these as natural or innate.

In this respect, the panopticon prison system is regarded as the perfect metaphor to explain how bodies are regimented and controlled in contemporary culture. Indeed, make-over narratives (both fiction films and television make-over shows) nearly always reproduce the system of the panopticon in order to remind the spectator of how the body is (should be) disciplined. One extremely popular television make-over show, *10 Years Younger*, dramatises the system of panoptic surveillance and discipline at the very start of every episode. The premise of the show is that it finds a body that has been wayward and has neglected to adhere to the rules of "appropriate" performance and iconography. Usually, this is a body that has been doing "harmful" practices such as smoking, drinking too much, neglecting oral hygiene and dentistry or (and this is often represented as the ultimate horror) failing to wear a sunscreen to protect the skin from the sun's ageing rays. Similarly, it may be a body that doesn't adhere to the rules of gender performance, and the show often features women who dress in masculine fashions or fail to remove facial hair or (and again this is another horror for the show) *dare* to appear in public without wearing make-up. The programme immediately aims to make the participant aware of the fact that her (and it usually is a woman – see below) actions are wrong. She must learn that she is under the constant surveillance of culture and that culture disapproves of her performances and/or iconography. The show accomplishes this by making the unfortunate woman stand in a public space (usually the street or a shopping centre) and inviting members of the general public to make insensitive comments about her. If her skin is sun damaged, somebody will point this out. The public's comments are then replayed to the woman and by the end of the introductory section of the show, the woman should be left feeling that she is too ugly to live. The point of this ordeal is to remind the woman that she is in a metaphoric version of the panopticon and to learn that her body is under the constant surveillance of the public. She may have been deceiving herself that people did not notice her sun-damaged skin or "inappropriate" grooming but this activity should remind her that she is under constant scrutiny from culture. Like the inmate of the panopticon, it is hoped that she will then become a self-policing subject and adhere to the rules of appearance and gender performance and, for example, stop unprotected sunbathing or smoking forty cigarettes a day – or whatever her "crime" has been. Although the show is entitled *10 Years Younger*, it often has nothing to do with age at all, and in fact many of the episodes are just about forcing bodies to perform more "appropriate" femininity or learning to police or regiment their bodies into more "acceptable" fashions. It's worth noting that although *10 Years Younger* is certainly attempting to instil a sense of self-surveillance in the subject, the show is also laced with a taste of premodern torture. The exhibition of the woman in the public space connotes the ritual of premodern torture comparable to locking someone in the stocks or giving someone a public flagellation. Indeed, it's remarkable that makeover shows are perhaps the only spectacle in which a public "assault" of a woman's body is permitted and sometimes even praised. This tradition, arguably, started with Trinny and Susannah (original presenters of the make-over show *What Not to Wear*) who became famous for the way they would often grab the subject's breasts and, on one occasion, even placed a hand up the woman's skirt and removed her knickers (as the Visible Panty Line was deemed too offensive to the dress). This motif has continued with Gok Wan presenting *How to Look Good Naked* in which he often feels a woman's breasts and remarks on how she has great "bangers" which need to be emphasised in the dress or blouse. Although Wan is openly gay identified, and therefore the action is "identified" as non-sexual, it is still a male body grabbing a woman's breasts and often this action takes place in a public space. The significance of this action is intensified by the fact that Wan often uses "laddist" terminology, such as "bangers", to refer to a woman's breasts (see Richardson and Wearing 2014).

As the above examples have shown, make-over shows still focus on the female body as the subject requiring revision and repair. Although male bodies do feature in make-over shows, they are certainly not as common as female bodies and do not undergo the same degree of physical invasion and aggressive surgical revision. Often a male body is simply required to tidy up, get a hair-cut and start shaving. In other words, male make-overs tend to require simply more attention to basic hygiene and grooming while female participants are subjected to extreme manipulation and surgical revision.

In this respect, feminist cultural theory has correctly pointed out that the metaphor of the panopticon (regimenting bodies' iconography and performance) is *gendered*. As Sandra Bartky famously argued:

> The woman who checks her make-up half a dozen times a day to see if her foundation has caked or her mascara run, who worries that the wind or rain may spoil her hairdo has become just as surely as the inmate of the Panopticon, a self-policing subject, a self committed to a relentless self surveillance.
>
> (1990: 80)

Although male bodies are certainly becoming victims of the tyranny of beauty, it has not reached the same level experienced by female bodies in contemporary culture. (Exceptions to this do exist. Metropolitan gay culture is, of course, famous for its brutal body fascism (see Richardson and Wearing 2014).)

The effects of this panoptic gaze in contemporary culture cannot be underestimated in relation to body image and performance. First, this gaze "normalises". Through establishing what is considered appropriate and inappropriate, a standard of "normal" is created. Take the example of ageing addressed in the show *10 Years Younger*. The happy ending of the show is when the make-over subject is presented to the public who are asked to identify the body's age. If the body is identified as younger than its biological age then the make-over is deemed to have been a success. However, this representation raises the expectations of the appearance of a specific age. A 50-year-old woman is deemed to look "acceptable" after various invasive (and expensive) cosmetic procedures ranging from aesthetic dentistry to cosmetic surgery. In other words, this show changes the discourse of ageing in that an untreated 50-year-old is deemed intolerable at the start of the show and only a surgically manipulated 50-year-old (the body at the end of the show) is deemed acceptable. Similarly, the media's gaze on celebrity and star culture normalises by establishing standards of weight, age iconography and fashion which are taken as the norm rather than as an exception. A 50-year-old celebrity's body is rarely ever praised as being an exception for his/her age but is simply identified as something which is representative of "good" or "appropriate" ageing. In other words, something to which we should all aspire to.

Second, the gaze homogenises. Through the process of standardisation/normalisation, there is little room for any variation outside of this "norm". This is perhaps most obvious if we consider racial or ethnic variations. If we consider the media's representation of celebrities who are not Caucasian, we often see a trajectory of homogenisation taking place. For example, the singer/actress Jennifer Lopez, although always identified in terms of her Latina-ness, has been subject to a process of homogenisation over recent years. Lopez's hair has become lighter and straighter, her skin appears considerably fairer and her jewellery and make-up have become less Latin. Therefore, although Lopez's "Latina-ness" is still being emphasised (there is still considerable focus on her butt – the fetishised body part of much Latin American culture, thought to exemplify feminine beauty and sexuality), the rest of her iconography has been changed in order to make her conform to an homogenous (Anglo-American) view of feminine beauty.

Finally, this gaze idealises. On one level this seems a very obvious point as culture has always exalted the ideal. We have only to consider the tradition of art, dating back to classical statuary, to see that there has always been an interest in the "ideal" human form. However, the key issue to stress here is that not only is there a narrow prescript of what is deemed ideal but that this has evolved and developed in recent years. Students often remark that bodies deemed "ideal" in previous generations would now be dismissed as out of shape or even fat. The beautiful nudes of classical art are now viewed as too fleshy and untoned. Even Michelangelo's *David* would be criticised nowadays for not being ripped enough. Most importantly, however, the notion of the ideal has shifted. Instead of being the realm of the divine or the impossible, it is now set as the standard to which bodies should aspire. Chapter 3 will look in more detail at the diet/fitness and beauty industry but at this point it is worth emphasising that the ideal is not simply something at which we should marvel (as was – arguably – the case with classical art/ statuary) but is now something which we *should* all be capable of achieving for ourselves (see chapters 3 and 4). The media delights in images of celebrity bodies when they are out of shape, ungroomed and looking very unspecial. The message of these images is that if the celebrities can manage to look "ideal" at certain points then we should also be able to attain that level of excellence. If the celebrities are, in fact, like the rest of us and look average at points in the year, then we should also be able to attain their levels of beauty through dedication to the regimes of specific body projects. One of the most popular magazine stories in contemporary culture is a story which details how the reader can also have the figure/physique of a specific celebrity through following a specific regime or diet. If they can attain the realm of the ideal, then so can we.

RESISTANCE

The previous section has detailed how the body is involved in a political field; how the gaze of contemporary culture aims to regiment bodies into "appropriate" performances and, in doing so, normalises, homogenises and idealises a certain image. However, where there is power there is always resistance and when resistance takes place it tends to be performed through the body. A teenager's first act of rebellion, against parental or school authority, will nearly always be manifested via the body. Very often an initial act of resistance will be to style or colour the hair in a fashion deemed unacceptable by parents or school. The next stage would usually be some form of unsanctioned piercing (nose, eyebrow) and then a tattoo. Of course, these acts all have different implications in terms of permanence. An unconventional hairstyle (even one that has been coloured) will only last a limited period while a tattoo is a much bigger gesture due to its permanency.

Obviously, the teenager who colours his/her hair bright green feels it is a symbol of resistance to the controlling, disciplining gaze of the school and, as such, feels that he/she is being transgressive. However, an important question to bear in mind when considering the politics of bodily transgression is 'how transgressive is transgression?' (Wilson 1993). The transgressor feels that he/she is transgressing the rules or boundaries of propriety and making a challenge, a form of resistance, to the discipline of the establishment. Yet it is worth remembering three points about the act of transgression. First, the transgressor is, by the very act of transgression, showing a form of respect for the disciplinary control. For example, only a teenager who is acutely aware of the rules of required hairstyle in the school would try to challenge it. If the teenager were indifferent to the requirements of hairstyle then he/she would not bother transgressing. In other words, transgression always affirms a respect for the normative by its very act of transgression. A popular example is the act of blasphemy in that only someone who credits Christianity would bother using God's name in such a fashion. For someone who was a true atheist, the act of blasphemy would mean nothing at all (see Wilson 1993).

Second, it is worth considering how long the act of transgression can be sustained. If we take the example of unconventional hair within the context of the school, we can see that the student who has challenged the normative style required for the school by, say, dying the hair a lurid colour has, indeed, transgressed from the normative into another category. This undoubtedly challenges the regime in the school. However, this student has now moved into a subcultural grouping of students who have dyed their hair and is now simply part of the norm within that particular subculture. Like the dominant culture, this subculture of "dyed-hair students" will have its own rules, regulations and requirements, and so this student is now simply part of the norm in that subculture and therefore no longer transgressive. If the student wished to continue making an act of defiance, he/she would have to do something else such as further enhancements to the hair or perhaps some other form of body modification such as piercing or tattooing. In other words, transgression can only have limited power as it may well defy the dominant but only moves the subject into a subcultural group in which this defiance is read simply as the norm.

Third, and perhaps most importantly, hegemonic culture will always respond to these acts of subcultural defiance by incorporating their styles and aesthetics into the mainstream. Take, for example, the style of punk which developed in the 1970s. Punk was, in many ways, a bricolage of all the movements of youth rebellion from the previous decades. It identified itself in terms of anti-authoritarianism and demonstrated its ideologies through its fashion and iconography. Hair was often dyed lurid colours and spiked while clothes were often ripped and torn and held together with safety pins and sticky tape (see chapter 5). Undoubtedly this was a challenge to regimes of normativity but then this style was adopted by various designers, most notably Vivienne Westwood and Jean Paul Gaultier, who turned elements of this iconography into haute couture. Arguably, something similar can be seen occurring in the culture of tattooing. Getting a visible tattoo was once an extremely transgressive act but given its ever-increasing rise in popularity it is becoming much more mainstreamed. Chapter 5 will detail similar examples in relation to body modification, focusing on bodybuilding as a case study. Competitive-level bodybuilding has had to evolve and become ever more extreme due to mainstream culture's embrace of the activity. In the Victorian era, audiences marvelled at the physique of the "first" bodybuilder: Eugen Sandow. When we show representations of Sandow to our students now, they remark that he has the average, moderately developed physique that could be seen in the majority of fashion advertisements or even on the gym floor of any bodybuilding gym.

RESISTANCE IS FUTILE?

As the last section has explained, challenging the "norm" poses three problems. First, the very act of resistance demonstrates a respect for the authority against which it is rebelling. Second, transgression moves the body into another subculture in which this body is now simply the "norm". Third, mainstream culture will adopt codes and conventions of resistance and, through processes of revision, will normatise them. In this respect, is resistance futile?

Although culture maintains control of bodies, throughout history there have always been moments of resistance and transgression in which ideologies of the "normal" have been challenged. The philosopher Mikhail Bakhtin, although famous for his writing on the philosophy of language, is also respected for his consideration of the social activity of the medieval carnival (1984). Carnivals were periods in which there was a temporary suspension of the codes of propriety and decorum. At times of carnival, people would perform actions that would be unsanctioned at other times of the year. People would drink and eat to excess, standards of decorum would be overruled and respect for gender, social and political hierarchies would be temporarily suspended. For example, one popular activity at the carnival might be the Feast of Fools (a type of alternative beauty pageant) in which the "ugliest" fool would be crowned the winner. In this respect, carnival was about inverting the norm and overthrowing regimes of discipline and control. Bakhtin argued that three main agendas were at work in creating the spirit of the carnival. First, carnival permitted the mingling of people who would, at other times, be separated by class, gender or age. At these festivals the rich would also mix with the poor. Second, carnival was about challenging the ideologies of Christianity, which was very much the dominant power at that period. Carnivals would take place in cathedral courtyards and, for example, would flout the Christian teachings of asceticism and modesty. Third, and most importantly, carnival permitted eccentric and inappropriate forms of expression – especially in relation to the body. People could dress inappropriately and style their bodies in unconventional ways.

However, carnival was a temporary period of suspension and, after the carnival was finished, "normal" life should resume the following day. Yet the spectacle of carnival should leave a lasting impression on the participant as the suspension of normative regimes *should* force the subject to consider what actually *is* normal. A spectacle such as the Feast of Fools should make the onlooker reflect on what actually is deemed to be beautiful and appropriate. In this respect, the carnival had, to a certain extent, the power to make people question the rules and regulations of culture. The name given to any activity which replicates those strategies is "carnivalesque" and we can talk about certain activities and practises as carnivalising.

As we will see in subsequent chapters, moments of carnivalesque do continue in contemporary culture. For example, consider an activity examined in more detail in chapter 5: the bodybuilding competition/show. This is a strange cultural practice in which an audience – mostly men and *arguably* heterosexually identified – extract considerable pleasure from gazing upon the performances of nearly nude men on the stage. This activity is carnivalising gender regimes (it's an activity of men openly objectifying and appraising other men's bodies) but is challenging normative iconography through the extremity of the bodies and also basic ideas of decorum in relation to clothing/nakedness. Similarly, the media fascination with extreme bodies can inspire a sense of the carnival. Take, for example, the media's fascination with the late Lolo Ferrari – a "celebrity" who was famous for having the most surgically augmented breasts in the world. Rumoured to have had between eighteen and twenty-five operations on her breasts, Ferrari was listed in the 1999 *Guinness Book of World Records* for having the biggest breast implants. Arguably, anyone watching Ferrari may experience a sense of the carnivalesque in that Ferrari's surgically augmented body, although having attained the dimensions of a schoolboy's erotic doodle, would force any spectator to consider if this is actually "beautiful". Although Ferrari's dimensions approximated a Barbie doll, when presented with these "ideal" dimensions – realised in the flesh – is it actually "desirable"? In this respect, Ferrari *could* be read as embodying a type of feminist critique of tyrannies of beauty. Through her exaggeration of the "ideal" female form, her appearance is challenging – carnivalising – discourses of what is deemed erotic or desirable. (For an excellent analysis of Ferrari, see Jones 2008.)

However, as chapter 4 will consider, hegemonic culture maintains a defence strategy against bodies that resist normative ideologies, and try to challenge/question them through carnivalising processes, and that strategy is "enfreakment". While the media may delight in representing unusual bodies, it is becoming more common that these bodies are displayed in accordance with the strategies usually found in the archaic spectacle of the "freak" show. Lolo Ferrari, for example, far from challenging discourses of feminine iconography and beauty, was often "contained" within the discourse of "freak". Yet, as chapter 4 will argue, it is also possible to consider that the spectacle of the "freak" show is making a comment on the regimes of the normal, asking the spectator to consider what is beautiful, appropriate or normal by making us wonder if we are really all that different from the "freak" body on display.

This chapter has tried to explain that power is a capillary force which cannot be reduced to a basic formula of a powerful person or group that controls another group. Similarly, discipline is not simply a matter of exerting force on the body but works in a more subtle fashion through the cultural gaze which makes the spectator internalise regimes of "appropriateness". Although the possibility for resistance exists, it will always be met with opposition. Nevertheless, there are moments when challenges can be sustained and there is a (re)consideration of the ideas of the normal. Such moments of challenge will the subject of the case studies in the next three chapters.

RECOMMENDED READING

Bakhtin, Mikhail (1984) *Rabelais and His World* (trans. H. Iswolsky) (Bloomington: Indiana University Press)

A very influential text which introduced the concept of the carnivalesque to contemporary academic debates and also asked scholars to consider the politics of the grotesque. Bakhtin argues that the carnival could be a site where societal norms are inverted and challenged and the grotesque body can be read as not simply a body of excess but one that is rebellious and rejecting authority.

Bartky, Sandra Lee (1990) *Femininity and Domination: Studies in the Phenomenology of Oppression* (London: Routledge)

One of the most important books in contemporary feminism and Body Studies, Bartky analyses the oppression of femininity through a Foucauldian critical lens. This text is important for demonstrating how feminist cultural theory can be mobilised to address issues of oppression and domination in contemporary culture and how the subject has internalised these regimes.

Foucault, Michel (1977) *Discipline and Punish: The Birth of the Prison* (trans. Alan Sheridan) (Harmondsworth: Penguin)

Arguably the founding text of Body Studies, *Discipline and Punish* remains a key text for scholars of gender, sexuality and the body. This book is one of the first to stress the constructed nature of the body and how it is implicated in discourses of power, control and management.

BODY IMAGE
BEAUTY AND AGE(ING)

In this chapter we want to consider the effects of the multibillion pound business of the beauty industry. For some critics, beauty is sold as the central concern and focus for women and such debates are discussed in chapter 2. Such readings as this can be seen in the context of docile bodies. Yet other critics have suggested that women have far more agency in their consumption of idealised images of beauty. This chapter will briefly examine the variety of messages that circulate around such themes and the way that they suggest the female body as some-*thing* that must always be perfected.

ORIGINS OF PERFECTION

In ancient Greece, it was the Greek sculptor Polyclitus who was the first artist to devise a canon for the human body with the idea that certain proportions would operate as a model of perfection. As Kenneth Clark noted, use of mathematical formulae to describe and to devise ideal proportions had existed many years before the classical age, and it underlay all Greek natural philosophy, but it was Polyclitus who codified it for the human body (1957: 33). According to Charles Freeman, Polyclitus was likely influenced by Pythagoras' hypothesis that ideal numbers and proportions lay behind all physical things (1999: 258). Polyclitus thus devised a canon of the body that, as Claude Laisne reports, assembled a 'fixed series of proportions, relating the parts of the body to the whole' (1995: 117). Laisne continues: 'Thus the height of the head was one seventh of the total height of the body, and half the length of the legs, of the torso and the width of the shoulders' (117). For Greek sculptors like Polyclitus, beauty was dependent on numerical analysis, and as George L. Hersey explains: 'Like so many of his contemporaries, Polyclitus believed that numbers ought to govern the human form because numbers and their rational sequence contain innate moral and perhaps magical powers. One word for this power was "symmetry"' (1996: 44). Symmetry is a particularly important concept for the beauty industry. Its roots reside in the cultures of ancient Greece and Egypt where there was a theory of beauty and maths referred to as the "golden ratio". The golden ratio can be particularly found in an attractive face, as one account proposes:

> The human head forms a Golden Rectangle with the eyes at the mid-point. The mouth and nose can each be placed at Golden Sections of the distance between the eyes and the bottom of the chin. With this information it is possible to construct a human face with dimensions exhibiting the Golden Ratio. This is exactly how some modern surgeons are creating beauty.
>
> (Sriraman, Freiman and Lirette-Pitre 2009: 126)

However, as chapter 4 will explain, this notion of the physical "ideal" was, until fairly recently, thought to be the preserve of art. Although there have always been representations of the "ideal" body (paintings or sculptures of gods and goddesses), the idea that this could be attainable for humans did not occur until the nineteenth century. It wasn't until the development of increasing industrialisation and workforces that a need arose to account for people in terms of workforce statistics (see L. Davis 1995). As such, the idea of the body which was "appropriate" for work – the well-managed body – came into existence and, as a result, the idea of the norm became linked to the "ideal". Now the "ideal" body was not simply the vision of sculptors but the body that could contribute to the socio-economic culture (see chapter 4 for further elaboration).

THE "GROOMING" INDUSTRY: THE BATTLE FOR WOMEN'S BODIES

Grooming is an activity done by both animals and humans. Its role is in keeping one healthy and clean, yet it equally functions as a means to maintain social and cultural relations. We groom ourselves via a variety of methods: perhaps at the beginning of the day washing with soap; using exfoliants; applying a face mask; using moisturising creams or lotions; utilising a toner; putting on lipstick/ lip liner/lip gloss; applying mascara and foundation; or having more specialist treatments such as Botox or a chemical skin peel. However, grooming is a distinctly gendered activity with women expected to engage in much more detailed and intricate grooming processes than men.

The beauty industry is a multibillion dollar business which is controlled by just a handful of multinationals that emerged in the first half of the twentiethth century, namely: Estée Lauder, L'Oréal, Shiseido and Unilever. Fierce debate continues about whether such a business positions women as objects of consumption and consumerism, or conversely, as subjects who can determine their own subjectivity. Some might argue that beauty is a conduit for reproduction; our looks attract a mate and, in this sense, it seems "natural". But there are many others who see beauty as a political tool in which men get to realise their own sexual fantasies while, also, working against women's sense of self and self-worth.

In her book *Bodies*, Susie Orbach remarks how '[w]hether followers of fashion or health trends or not, we take for granted that looking good for ourselves will make us feel good'. As she continues, 'yet there is a subtle tracery of outside urgings which works on us, creating a new and often dissatisfied relationship with our bodies' (2009: 2). For Orbach, there is a strong cultural belief in a 'perfectible body' which, ironically, has made the body increasingly 'unstable' and 'a site of serious suffering and disorder' (2). With the ubiquity of pernicious images of airbrushed perfection, young people (women *in particular*) have become increasingly focused on, and deeply dissatisfied with, the appearance of their bodies. Germaine Greer comments that '[e]very woman knows that, regardless of her other achievements, she is a failure if she is not beautiful' and, hence, 'sophisticated marketing will have persuaded the most level-headed woman to throw money away on chemical preparations containing ... anything real or phoney that might fend off her imminent collapse into hideous decrepitude' (2000: 23, 28). There is an enormous amount of pressure (especially) on women to relentlessly pursue attractiveness and youth and so the illnesses anorexia, bulimia and body dysmorphic disorder are often seen as the disheartening result of this attempt to live up to cultural expectations.

One of the best known texts to analyse the detriment of women through idealised images of beauty is Naomi Wolf's *The Beauty Myth*. This book was – and still is – a hugely influential feminist work on femininity in the 1990s and discusses how the media presents images of women which make them feel deeply unhappy with themselves. Wolf calls this 'the beauty myth' where '[w]omen must want to embody it and men must want to possess women who embody it' (1991: 12). For Wolf, 'beauty' is a bogus 'currency system' which supports male patriarchy through an oppressive power structure and is primarily 'about men's institutions and institutional power' (13). In other words, the beauty industry coerces women to focus on their bodies while curtailing the huge inroads in feminist advancement that have been made by women. Wolf does not argue for women not to want to feel beautiful, but the problem for her resides in when women feel forced to wear make-up so as to not lose a job or just to feel womanly; many women feel they cannot leave the house without some application of make-up. In her conclusion, Wolf contemplates life post-beauty myth and writes:

> How might women act beyond the myth? Who can say? Maybe we will let our bodies wax and wane, enjoying the variations on a theme, and avoid pain because when something hurts us it begins to look ugly to us. Maybe we will adorn ourselves with real delight, with the sense that we are gilding the lily. Maybe the less pain women inflict on our bodies, the more beautiful our bodies will look to us. Perhaps we will forget to elicit admiration from strangers, and find we don't miss it; perhaps we will await our older faces with anticipation, and be unable to see our bodies as a mass of imperfections, since there is nothing on us that is not precious. Maybe we won't want to be the "after" anymore.
>
> (291)

Conversely, some feminists take the opposite view of how beauty and fashion regimes are read as a bête noire for women. In her book *Fresh Lipstick*, Linda M. Scott, argues against other established voices in the field – most notably Susan Faludi, Susan Bordo, Naomi Wolf and Lois Banner – who, unlike her, passionately argue that 'American women have struggled under the patriarchal power of the fashion business' (2005: 2). Scott makes the point early in her book that it's incorrect to label the beauty and fashion industry as simply an oppressive patriarchy since various women have been key players in the business (a point also raised by others such as G. Jones 2010). Yet more importantly, the thesis of her discussion is an argument with the anti-beauty line which claims that women are seen as sex objects whose devotion to looking beautiful side tracks them from the more imperative issues of the mind. As Scott states at the end of her book, '[Women] should not waste time quibbling over what to wear to the [feminist] conflict' (2005: 331). In this respect, Scott suggests that such feminist debates over clothing and fashion are, often, obsessing over the irrelevant.

However, it is important to remember that Scott is debating issues such as fashion and make-up rather than extreme surgical interventions which reshape and remodel the female body. Similarly, these debates are located within our contemporary context of postfeminist culture and although there is considerable discussion as to what actually constitutes postfeminism, most critics agree that a postfeminist identification is the luxury of Western, middle-class white women who have attained a degree of success within metro-politan settings. As such, these women can "afford" to reclaim (often in an ironic fashion) early performances of prefeminist femi-ninity because their affluence and socio-economic success permits this (see Gill 2007; McRobbie 2009; Negra 2009).

Likewise, in a study on women's consumption of Ann Summers products, Marl Storr shares some of Scott's ideas about women not simply being disempowered by fashion products – though this time at the more extreme end of the fashion/taste spectrum. On the one hand, there is some element of sexual liberation for women which Storr views 'as a post-feminist dynamic which forges gender iden-tifications around images of "useless" men and liberated women' (2003: 216). Yet on the other, serious issues around "sexual inequality" are left not only "intact", but "unacknowledged". In one sense, if beauty is not a "natural" state, but some-*thing* achieved through buying into the beauty business, then women are fashioning their own identities. From this, some feminists see the way that women can play with roles through fashion and make-up as something that can be read as liberating. Nevertheless, as Storr demonstrates, women are perhaps again playing into notions of a normative femininity whose notions of beauty are male defined. There is the palpable sense here that women are unable to slip away from the gendered panoptic gaze discussed in chapter 2. Indeed, as Joan Copjec summarises, 'the panoptic gaze defines *perfectly* the situation of the woman under patriarchy' (1989: 54). Therefore, despite all the elements of supposed sexual liberation, independence and empowerment, Storr may leave us feeling that Ann Summers is probably not the path to sexual equality.

NIP 'N' TUCK

Natasha Walter, author of the acclaimed text *Living Dolls*, takes a dim view of a culture where breast implants, fake nails, spray tans and a myriad of other alterations and additions to the female body are suggested by the media to be liberating and empowering. For Walter they are blatantly not. In the opening section of her book, Walter narrates how toy dolls such as Barbie and Bratz seem to be 'taking over [young] girls' lives' (2010: 2). Launched in 1959 by Mattel in America, Barbie is a toy which needs little, if any, introduction. Like Barbie, the Bratz doll also stems from California (through MGM Entertainment), though the toy's origins are much more nascent. Both Barbie and Bratz have resulted in numerous spin-offs through the now frequent practice of synergy. As Walter reflects: 'The brilliant marketing strategies of these brands are managing to fuse the doll and the real girl in a way that would have been unthinkable a generation ago' (2). Walter observes how the body project 'of grooming, dieting, and shopping [now] aims to achieve the bleached, waxed, tinted look of a Bratz or Barbie doll' (2).

Correspondingly, comparisons can be made with the porn industry. Walter remarks that the image of female sexuality to which we now aspire 'has become more than ever defined by the terms of the sex industry' (2010: 3). Indeed, such a comment fits into the notion of a wider cultural sexualisation that Brian McNair calls a 'pornographication of the mainstream' (2002: 12). This porno-graphication is illustrated by a culture which can claim that pole dancing is "exercise", where porn stars feature as agony aunts in lads' magazines and there is a vogue for a Brazilian bikini wax (see Attwood 2009).

As featured in adult magazines and movies, female performers are sometimes characterised by surgically enhanced breasts. For most, this consists of an enlargement which, although often significant, is not extreme. However, some women in the porn profession have opted for enormous enlargements which represent an exaggerated aesthetic of femininity. Germaine Greer reports that *Playboy* maga-zine devised a test to define what constituted the "good" breast. As she writes: 'if a pencil slid under the breast of a standing woman stayed put, her breasts were saggy. A good breast by [this] definition does not sag'. Moreover, 'a woman who has good breasts is the one who has sizeable breasts that do not sag' (2000: 57).

Therefore, it has hardly surprising that contemporary culture has seen a huge increase in the number of women submitting to cos-metic surgery. Critical views on cosmetic surgery are divided. The most naïve view on cosmetic surgery would be to see it as simply another form of body modification (see chapter 5) but this view is, of course, ignoring the fact that body modifiers are attempting to challenge the idea of the norm while cosmetic surgery is trying to reproduce an extremely narrow idea of what is deemed "beautiful". Anne Balsamo points out that acts of cosmetic surgery upon the body are examples of 'techno-bodies' but ones in which the body is heavily *disciplined* and 'becomes an object of intense vigilance and control' (1999: 6). Key here is, as Balsamo comments, 'how certain technologies are ideologically shaped by the operation of gender interests and, consequently, how they serve to reinforce traditional gender patterns of power and authority' (10) (see chapter 2). Llewellyn Negrin echoes Balsamo's argument by arguing that the increasing popularity of cosmetic surgery should be viewed as making women victims of a patriarchal ideology which dictates how they should look based on male wishes and desires (2002: 21).

However, other critics have taken a more liberal view of the popularity of cosmetic surgery. Kathy Davis (1995) argues that cosmetic surgery *may* be read as an activity in which women acknowledge the pressures of contemporary culture but can be seen to be dealing with these socio-cultural demands in an active fashion. Such a view can read cosmetic surgery as women rising to the challenge of keeping young and beautiful in an appearance-oriented culture. Nevertheless, it must be remembered that liberal views on cosmetic surgery do little to account for why people (especially women) feel dissatisfaction with their appearance in the first place.

MALE BEAUTY

It might also be argued that many more men are now also victims of the beauty industry with rising numbers of males getting waxed, using numerous beauty products and sometimes resorting to surgery for everything from rhinoplasty (nose shaping) to tummy tucks (abdominoplasty). Indeed, the term "metrosexuality" has been coined (*arguably*, by the journalist Mark Simpson) to describe a type of young(ish) man, usually located within a metropolitan setting, who devotes a lot of time to beautifying his body and spending considerable amounts of money on contemporary fashion. Arguably, this sensibility is the result of metropolitan men adopting the paradigms of gay culture so that heterosexual men are now performing activities which were once thought to be the preserve of gay men such as going to gyms, shopping and enhancing their bodies (see Allen 2006; Berila and Choudhuri 2005; Miller 2005). However, this trend (if it really exists) seems to be located only in metropolitan settings and may be read as demonstrating masculine privilege rather than the obligation that women feel to conform to the tyranny of beauty.

Another argument has suggested that more pressure is now being placed upon men to regiment and sculpt their bodies' musculature. In *The Adonis Complex*, a very popular book examining the rise in male body image issues, Harrison Pope, Kate Phillips and Roberto Olivardia (2000) point out that figurines (action dolls) for young boys are now subject to the same hyperbolic iconography as can be seen in Barbie. For example, the G. I. Joe doll and *Star Wars* action figures have 'acquired the physiques of bodybuilders, with bulging "pecs" (chest muscles) and "delts" (shoulders)' (43). Compared with the same products from the 1970s, Pope, Phillips and Olivardia comment 'that the ideal male figure has evolved in only about thirty years from a normal and reasonably attainable figure … to a hugely muscular figure that we believe no man could attain without massive doses of steroids' (43–44). However, it is important to remember that these dolls are still marketed as action figures and the pleasure of playing with them is supposed to be the identification with their strength and ability rather than their beauty. These "steroided" action figures are sending a different message from, say, Barbie who is "sold" in terms of her beauty. In this respect, although it is fair to say that men are certainly now more subject to the tyranny of beauty than they were several decades ago, Kathy Davis is correct to point out that 'I find it difficult to see men as the new victims of the "beauty myth"' (2002: 51). Indeed, in terms of statistics, women still significantly outnumber men in submitting to cosmetic surgery in an effort to live up to this beauty ideal (2002) and, as Wolf makes clear, the troubling theme of the beauty industry is that beauty is *central* for a woman's identity. Therefore, while a metrosexual may devote considerable time and money to perfecting his appearance this is, arguably, a way of demonstrating masculine privilege and flaunting metropolitan wealth rather than the requirement to conform to paradigms of feminine beauty that is the case for women.

MEDIA IMAGES

Although heated debates continue regarding whether the media – and in particular, women's magazines – plays a significant role in making women deeply dissatisfied with their body image, it is difficult not to agree with David Gauntlett's comment that 'media images can play an unhelpful role' (2008: 202). For many women, magazines engender a sense of inadequacy. Magazine articles can make readers feel dissatisfied with who they are. Some pieces can make women feel guilty about what they've chosen in the great debate about whether they should have children or a career or manage both. Magazines present a contradictory set of ideas which present hyperthin models as a feminine ideal, which are widely criticised, and yet these are the images which are purchased by millions of female readers.

Yet, it's also important to stress the pleasures of such magazines and images. Women's magazines are a glossy, glamorous seduction where women can imagine themselves wearing the clothes and experiencing the lifestyles of celebrity. They are an enticement to the indulgent pleasure of curling up on one's own with a personal invitation to view the latest trends. It is a club where women can be part of the elite few and pick up gossip on the rich and famous. There's also a guilty pleasure in reading magazines. Maybe it's because they're packed with issues on beauty, health and relationships, all of which women like to feel they manage well enough. Maybe it's because many women will read horoscopes, gloat at problem pages, fill in quizzes and feel they ought to be doing something more productive with their time. As Gauntlett remarks, 'you can't really miss the fact that women's magazines speak the language of "popular feminism" – assertive, seeking success in work and relationships, demanding the right to both equality and pleasure' (205).

Nevertheless, Gauntlett flags up the deaths in 2006 of "size-zero" models Ana Carolina Reston and Luisel Ramos, both from hazardous dieting. As he writes, these high-profile casualties generated a great deal of debate about the dangers of "size zero", but it has not stopped the use of skinny models in the magazines (202–203). Such models highlight the often complex and perturbing relation many women have with food.

To conclude this section, arguments continue to rage about how culpable the beauty industry is in causing untold problems – both mental and physical – to women and, more recently, men as well. The effects of the beauty industry are continually questioned in the West but now other countries that are relatively new to Western ideals of physical beauty are entering into the debate. For example, Iran now has an ever-increasing number of rhinoplasty operations for women since many females want to look like the stars they watch in Western media, especially Hollywood cinema. In India female Bollywood stars have noticeably whiter skins than a few years ago, which feeds into a new cultural desire for skin lightening. Meanwhile, men in the West are becoming more comfortable with what's termed "manscaping" (or "grooming"), using a variety of beauty products, shaving their chests and even having "boyzilians" (a male Brazilian wax). Such actions have been seen as fitting in with an increasing dissatisfaction with the male body, a desire for the perfect physique (otherwise known as the "Adonis complex") and conformity to the contemporary sensibility of "metrosexuality".

For women who have been longer and more intensely under the spotlight of the beauty industry, the debates seem even more complex. To return to the topic of magazines, while men are often shown in women's magazines as figures of status and equality, in men's publications women are more often represented as sex objects serving men's (sexual) interests. It seems that for many feminist critics, the beauty industry plays out such an ideologically repressive fantasy against women's faces and bodies.

AGEING

"Ageing" is now a key topic in cultural studies. Its popularity may be due to the fact that growing "old" is something which *directly* affects everyone, unlike other identifications such as, say, ethnicity or disability. Provided we live long enough, we will all experience "old" age. Arguably, this is why gerontophobia (fear of ageing) is such a powerful anxiety in that it is not simply a fear of a quantified, minority group but a terror that, one day, we might become part of that group. In this respect, gerontophobia is not comparable to other forms of discrimination such as, say, racism. A racist might harbour terrible beliefs about a specific racial group but the racist does not hold any anxiety that, eventually, he/she will become part of that racial minority.

Like all identifications, ageing is not merely biological but cultural. Bodies will age biologically but how this is *identified* is culturally mutable and so what is deemed "old" will vary according to geographical and historical context. As Karen Stoddard points out, "'old" is different to each culture and to each time period, so that an American woman aged fifty in 1920 was considered old, while a woman of the same age in 1980 is considered middle-aged' (1983: 21). More importantly, how age is identified is inflected by our other cultural identifications such as sexuality, race, socio-economic class and, arguably the most important, gender (see next but one paragraph).

However, unlike other cultural identifications such as, say, sexuality, age is also *social* in that it is quantified by societal laws, giving it a precision which sexuality or class do not have. For example, in contemporary British culture when a person reaches a certain age he/she is given a bus pass and "labelled" an Old Age Pensioner.

Similarly, "young" people can obtain a Young Person's Travel Card and this can be used as an official testament that the body is socially quantified as "young". It is noteworthy that this quantification of age is deemed important within public spaces (especially transport systems) thus suggesting that socio-legal structures view the regimentation of bodies' age as the most important of social identifications. In this respect, ageing is not only a cultural identification but social qualification.

Much of the existing writing on ageing has, understandably, addressed feminist concerns of gender and sexuality. Ten years ago the gender studies mantra was "fat is a feminist issue" but has now become "*age* is a feminist issue". Biologically, men do not age any "better" than women but the physical signs of ageing are interpreted differently for masculinity than they are for femininity. For example, within linguistic discourses a man whose hair has turned grey is described as "distinguished" or a "silver fox". Such terms are not applicable to an image of ageing femininity. Indeed, most of the negative terms to describe ageing, such as "hag", "crone", "witch", "old bag", are only applicable to femininity. (There are negative terms to describe older men – the term "old git" is often used in British slang – but this term describes the man's cantankerousness rather than his appearance.)

Obviously the difference in the identification of ageing is related to the paradigm of "woman as body" (considered in detail in chapter 2). While women are valued in terms of their appearance, men (until fairly recently) have had the luxury of being able to be removed from the tyranny of beauty. A man's body is appraised in terms of what it can do rather than how it looks.

However, even within representations in which emphasising the beauty of the body is the image's agenda (advertising, for example) we still see a difference in the identification of ageing. While representations of female models will have the wrinkles airbrushed, advertisements using male models often allow the wrinkles to remain thus suggesting that lines on the male face are a signifier of masculine beauty. While many advertisements may airbrush a female model's wrinkles to such an extent that she has not even the slightest line on her skin, representations of male models will often allow the forehead lines to remain. Of course, this relates to the coding usually employed in the representation of the male body (see Dyer 1982). The male model often returns the gaze of the camera while wearing an intense facial expression, thus suggesting that the model's mind is involved in processes of thought/intellectual debate and therefore not simply a body to be gazed at. A male model's forehead lines seem to suggest he is musing on a complex subject and therefore reinforces the binary of masculinity associated with thought and reason while femininity is simply the body and emotion. However, what cannot be ignored is that it is deemed acceptable for male models to wear wrinkles on their faces but it is unacceptable in female models.

Given this type of media imagery, it is hardly surprising that ageing is discursively constructed as a "problem" for women. Many anti-ageing creams and lotions identify the signifiers of age as a "concern" that needs to be treated. Indeed, as Tasker and Negra point out, a recent advertisement simply identified age-defying cosmetic "treatments" as something that women *will* need to submit to rather than being an elective procedure (2007). In contemporary culture, it seems that defying the ageing process is a requisite of hegemonic femininity. The same is, arguably, not the case for men and, as Kathy Davis points out, when men are represented as submitting to cosmetic anti-ageing procedures they are usually identified as odd or even imbalanced (2002).

However, the exception here might be gay men and it is fair to say that the tyranny of ageing does apply more to gay men than to heterosexual men (see Jones and Pugh 2005; Sandberg 2008; Richardson and Wearing 2014). Having said that, the unashamed eroticisation of the older male body can be found in gay popular culture – especially pornography (see J. Mercer 2012). A blog such as *Silver Fox Men* (http://silverfoxmen.tumblr.com/ last accessed 29 April 2012) celebrates the sexiness of the older male body in softly (homo)erotic images. Although there are websites which eroticise the older female body, these sites are usually coded as perverse or even deviant.

Therefore, if age is coded as a "problem" for femininity, it is something which must be "treated" and, if it can be, disguised. However, here is the problem for ageing femininity in that disguising/treating female age can lead to the subject being identified as "mutton dressed as lamb". As Helle Rexbeye explains, "'Mutton dressed as lamb' has been a well known phenomenon at least since the eighteenth century describing women who act or dress much younger than prescribed by the cultural norms for their age ... . What seems just as important though, is that the phrase implies looking cheap – and has implicit references to prostitution' (Rexbeye and Povlsen 2007: 71). As Beverly Skeggs famously asserted, attaining normative femininity requires a considerable amount of labour but yet this labour *must* be concealed. If the labour is not disguised from view then the female body is identified as cheap and/or distasteful (see Skeggs 1997). This seems to be even more the case when the issue of age(ing) is involved. If the female body fails to mask the signs of ageing with sufficient skill then she is either identified as "cheap" or, even worse, as grotesque. Indeed, one of the media's favourite stereotypes has, and continues to be, the "ageing female grotesque". This is the body which is attempting to fulfil its obligation to disguise the ageing process yet it fails miserably. Two of the most popular ageing female grotesques in Hollywood have been Baby Jane Hudson from the cult horror *Whatever Happened to Baby Jane?* and Norma Desmond from *Sunset Boulevard* (see Chivers 2006). More recently, Hollywood has revived the ageing female grotesque with the (*arguably* ironic) representation of fairy-tale witches, obsessed with maintaining/regaining their youth, in the films *Stardust*, *The Brothers Grimm* and *Tangled* (see Cahill 2010). Understandably, given the popularity of this stereotype, much of the existing film and media scholarship has addressed the relationship that ageing female bodies on the screen hold to sexuality, sexual attractiveness and, of course, the dynamics of gendered spectatorship (see Andrews 2003; Chivers 2011; Dolan and Tincknell 2012; Jermyn 2013; Wearing 2007, 2009; Varies 2009; Whelehan 2009).

However, there is considerable debate among scholars as to how popular culture's image of the "ageing female grotesque" *may* be interpreted. One way of reading this image is as unadulterated misogyny, if not even the representation strategy discussed in chapter 4: enfreakment. As Kathryn Weibel argues (talking about actors such as Bette Davis and Joan Crawford), 'It is a shame that such actresses were not allowed to mature in films by portraying advanced wisdom which age brings, instead of presenting aging women as *freaks*' (1977: 112, emphasis added). While ageing male bodies are usually coded in terms of their wisdom and authority, ageing female bodies are subject to the strategy of enfreakment in which they become a source of ridicule and/or horror.

On the other hand, another strand of criticism would assert that it is possible to read a feminist-inspired challenge in popular culture's representation of ageing femininity as grotesque and/or monstrous. Catherine Silver, for example, argues that female 'ageing is increasingly understood as a form of resistance to the patriarchal order' (2003: 385, see also Greer 1992) in that it allows 'the lifting of social and symbolic controls around sexuality, femininity and family obligations' (387). In this argument, the ageing female body *enjoys* a liberation from the oppression of patriarchal culture as she is no longer conscripted to the regimes of hetero-patriarchal femininity. In this respect, Morey has argued that Baby Jane Hudson and Norma Desmond may be read as 'an expression of rage against [the] system' (2011: 107) in which the actors' extreme performances are critiquing the oppression of (ageing) femininity within patriarchy.

Finally, there are critics who have taken the queer/poststructural approach and have celebrated the representation of the ageing female grotesque because she 'transgresses and confounds all manner of social conventions from notions of gender propriety and decorum to received dictates about erotic desirability and appropriate sexual relationality' (Farmer 2000: 146–147). Martin Shingler, for example, in his analyses of Bette Davis's performances, has argued that Davis's representation of extreme characters, such as Baby Jane Hudson, can be praised for the way it 'exploited the ironies and ambiguities of gender' so that her 'masquerade of feminine comes remarkably close to that of female impersonation, to drag' (1995: 181). Baby Jane Hudson may be read as a *female* drag queen who, like a virtuoso drag artist, is drawing attention to the construction of femininity through caricaturing the norms of gender.

Indeed, this concept of "age drag" is often applicable to a number of ageing female celebrities who have managed to maintain careers in our youth-obsessed culture through their autocritique of their ageing bodies. The stand-up comedienne Joan Rivers, for example, constantly draws attention to her ageing body and how she attempts to fulfil her *obligations* of disguising the ageing process through a variety of cosmetic procedures. The model Janice Dickinson, arguably, performs a similar strategy in all her performances. Indeed, it could be argued that ageing female celebrities often employ the strategy usually associated with gay men – camp. As Andy Medhurst argued, camp is a 'strategy of defensive offensiveness' (1997) in which the subject is exaggerating, even caricaturing, elements which might be the source of ridicule and insult from someone else. By drawing attention to their ageing bodies, and the demands of patriarchal culture that they mask/disguise this process, celebrities such as Rivers and Dickinson are preventing the insult of "mutton dressed as lamb" or "ageing female grotesque" as they have already drawn attention to, and made fun of, this aspect of their own performances.

The other popular stereotype of ageing femininity is "senile old fool" or "dotty dear", a body which is conveniently contained within the rhetoric of the "politics of pity" – a representational strategy often found within the history of disability iconography. This body doesn't demonstrate the aggression and anger of the "ageing female grotesque" but is a softer image of "endearing" dottiness and closer to the established medical model of age which delineates age in terms of "frailty" rather than appearance. (In Western medicine, the subject is deemed frail not because of calendar years but because of the subject's ability to function within social circumstances.)

This stereotype signifies neediness and the idea of older bodies being in their "second childhood" which require the care and protection usually afforded to children. The genesis of this stereotype can be traced back to the destruction of society that occurred as a result of the atrocity of World War II. The loss of so many male soldiers (many of whom were husbands and fathers) shattered the family support system by leaving many women, in prefeminist 1950s society, without the financial and emotional support of their husbands and/or fathers. As such, older people – especially older women – began to be 'perceived as social problems' (Williams, quoted in Blaikie 1997: 637) and a burden on the State. As Williams argues, 'This perception informed and directed much of the picturing of older people that was to appear over the next 30 years' (637).

Indeed, this cinematic stereotype of the "senile old fool" is almost as common as the stereotype of the "ageing female grotesque". The "dotty dear" is often wedged into the narrative to provide a moment of comic relief (an excellent example is the "old dears" in the British comedy film *Clockwise*) in which a lull in narrative suspense is solved by introducing two senile women who serve no other purpose than being the comic relief comparable to the Shakespearian fool.

Therefore, given the wealth of "negative" images of ageing femininity in contemporary culture, it is hardly surprising that counter discourses of "appropriate" or "successful" ageing have been created (see Torres and Hammarström 2006; Rowe and Kahn 1997). Indeed, popular culture is now actively trying to promote images of "successful" ageing in film and television. Recent British cinema, such as *Quartet*, *The Best Exotic Marigold Hotel*, *The Queen*, *Ladies in Lavender*, *Calendar Girls* (to name a few), has presented films which have aimed to prettify old age, challenging both the stereotype of the monstrous grotesque and the frail, "dotty dear" (see Richardson, forthcoming). A number of these texts have been Heritage films, a middle-brow cinema which *may* be read as an unashamed exaltation of the heritage of British culture. In this respect, Blaikie argues that the older female bodies represented in these films can be read as 'exemplars of all that was good about the nation's past' (1997: 629).

One of the most popular cultural texts to have exalted ageing femininity has been the fashion photographer Ari Seth Cohen's remarkably successful blog *Advanced Style* (http://advancedstyle. blogspot.co.uk/ last accessed 29 January 2013). *Advanced Style* is different from other fashion blogs in that the bodies which Cohen photographs are all in their 70s, 80s and even 90s. These images of truly *gorgeous* older women very much support the ideology of "successful" or "appropriate" ageing. However, as Featherstone and Wernick (1995) point out, there is a definite bias in terms of socio-economic class in these types of representations as it seems only to be those who have either the class capital (the Bourdieu concept of "taste"), or the socio-economic privilege to engage in consumerist practices, who can identify in terms of "successful" ageing. For those less privileged, there seems to be reduced access to this identification.

CONCLUSION

In this chapter we have provided an introduction to the way women are invariably seen as some-*thing* that has to be improved.

While a few critics see the beauty industry as a space where women can be assertive and empowered, many others take quite the opposite view; for them, the real agenda of the beauty industry isn't sexual emancipation, it is about pleasing men and controlling women. We have also discussed some of the critical responses to ageing. There is the oft-used phrase "ageing gracefully" which suggests that one should not only maintain looking good, staying active and so forth, but it is also underlined by the strong desire *not* to age. In her book *Aged by Culture* (2004) Margaret Gullette discusses an incident at the Boston Museum of Science with a particular exhibit called "Face Aging" (4). Lines of children wait in turn to go into a booth to watch as their faces are speedily and spectacularly aged before their eyes. Interested in their reactions, Gullette approaches some of the children and is given a collective answer: 'I don't want to get old'. She remarks that '[t]hey had nothing to add'. Nonetheless, we suggest there is a great deal to add. The topic of ageing deserves the current level of deep critical interest as it helps us come to terms with not only ourselves, but also those around us who remind each of us of our imminent future.

RECOMMENDED READING

BEAUTY (GENERAL)

Wolf, Naomi (1991) *The Beauty Myth: How Images of Beauty Are Used Against Women* (London: Vintage)

A highly influential text, *The Beauty Myth* considers how female oppression still operates in our supposed era of postfeminist emancipation. Wolf argues that women may no longer be oppressed as they were several decades ago but that the tyranny of beauty still subjects the female body to regimes of discipline and control.

COSMETIC SURGERY

Davis, Kathy (1995) *Reshaping the Female Body* (New York: Routledge)

A key text in the cultural studies literature on cosmetic surgery. Davis articulates an argument from a liberal feminist perspective in her analysis of elective cosmetic surgery in the Netherlands. This was one of the first texts to offer a nuanced examination of the politics of elective cosmetic surgery, arguing that it is too simplistic to read the activity as a monolithic power manipulating the female body.

Heyes, Cressida and Jones, Meredith (eds) (2009) *Cosmetic Surgery: A Feminist Primer* (Farnham: Ashgate)

An excellent collection which has been assembled by two internationally respected scholars on body image. This text collects the key feminist writings on the activity and guides the reader through the range of critical perspectives offered on elective cosmetic surgery.

AGEING

Dolan, Josephine and Tincknell, Estella (2012) *Ageing Femininities: Troubling Representations* (Cambridge: Cambridge Scholar Publishing)

A recent edited collection which assembles scholarship from leading scholars of age and ageing. *Ageing Femininities* analyses a range of cultural texts and guides the reader through the main areas that are key to these debates: the historical "invention" of "old age"; transgression and resistance and how "old" is negotiated in contemporary, postfeminist culture with an analysis of cultural icons such as Madonna, Dolly Parton and Helen Mirren.

Richardson, Niall (forthcoming) *Ageing Femininity: Representations of Older Women in Cinema* (London: I. B. Tauris)

This forthcoming contribution to the already extensive scholarship on ageing considers the politics of "age-affirmative" representations – media which aims to "prettify" age and exalt a particular ideology of "successful ageing". Underpinned by a Foucauldian critique, the text considers the dangerous politics of "affirmation" drawing parallels with how earlier media have performed similar strategies for other minority groups such as queer culture and disability.

Stoddard, Karen M. (1983) *Saints and Shrews: Women and Aging in American Popular Culture* (London: Greenwood Press)

One of the first, and most influential, texts to consider the representation of ageing femininity in popular media. Stoddard's analyses – particularly of classical Hollywood – should be key foundational reading for any scholars of age and ageing.

Sadie Wearing (forthcoming) *Age, Gender and Sexuality in Contemporary Culture*

Written by an internationally respected scholar of age and ageing, this monograph considers representations and theorisations of the ageing body in contemporary popular culture exploring the intersections of discourses of race, class, gender and sexuality in shifting conceptualisations of age.

MONSTROSITY, ENFREAKMENT AND DISABILITY

'The extraordinary body is fundamental to the narratives by which we make sense of ourselves and the world.'

(Garland Thomson 1996: 1)

The previous chapter considered contemporary culture's obsession with ideals of beauty: the culture of "beauty-ism". In contrast, this chapter analyses the other side of the coin and considers bodies that are deemed *not* to fit into narrow regimes of beauty or normativity. Here we enter the very sensitive debates of considering bodies that, in the past, have been ostracised from mainstream culture and labelled "monsters" or "freaks" and, more recently, identified within the category of disability.

As the last chapter has pointed out, there are innumerable television shows devoted to the management and regulation of body image in which the spectator is told what to wear, how to look, how to age, what is an "appropriate" weight – in short, how to conform. However, popular media has also evidenced an obsession with peering at bodies which, for a variety of reasons, are not identified as conforming to these ideals. While a great deal of popular culture is devoted to the regulation of the body, the policing of the body into "appropriate" image through make-over shows and advertising, the other side of popular culture has been a resurgence in the archaic spectacle of enfreakment. Arguably, the archaic spectacle of the "freak" show is still very much in popularity but has simply disguised itself in a variety of different formats (see Richardson 2010). Indeed, it is fair to say that a considerable amount of television is given over to shows which delight in extreme bodies – bodies which do not conform to the canon of the ideal. If spectators gaze in awe at perfected bodies, they stare, bug-eyed in amazement, at bodies which, for a variety of reasons, fail to match up to culture's ideal.

This chapter will consider the history of the representation of the un-ideal body and, like the other chapters, will relate these theories to relevant examples from Anglo-American popular culture. It will consider how unusual bodies were first identified as "monsters". It will then analyse how the "monster" became a "freak" and finally consider the politics of the identification of disability.

"MONSTERS"

The word "monster" derives from the Latin verbs *monstrare* (to show) or *monere* (to warn) because the earliest "monsters" were considered to be omens, warnings or prophecies. Within all stories of the great civilizations (Greco-Roman to Christian) there have been "monsters" and mythical creatures who have been read as godly forecasts – either showing the power of God/gods or warning of things to come. Indeed, until the Age of Enlightenment (when civilization made advances in science), "monsters" were simply read as a sign of the divine. Ambroise Paré's sixteenth-century text read "monsters" as direct signals from God (trans. Janis L. Pallister 1982). According to Paré, "monsters" could function in two different ways: they were either something which celebrated the glory of God, or were the very opposite and represented the wrath of God. "Monsters" were either a reason for celebration or a source of terror. For example, the Bible contains some truly terrifying "monsters" who were sent to punish people for their sins. The Book of Revelations details an utterly horrific beast – a creature with seven heads and ten horns – who was sent to punish the disobedient people (Revelations 13:1, 17:3). This beast was a warning of the wrathful power of God; how he could – and would – punish the people if they did not obey his command.

On the other hand, some "monsters" were symbols of the divine love of God – something which should suggest the glory of right-eousness. For example, the mythical creature of the unicorn is represented in divine iconography as the symbol of Christ. Many medieval tapestries and paintings (the most famous example is in the *Book of Kells*) represent the Madonna cradling the unicorn on her lap, in a pose that prefigures the divine Pietà in which she would hold the dying Christ. (This connection between unicorns and the body of Christ is why the collective noun for a group of unicorns is a blessing of unicorns.)

Indeed, many of the "monsters" featured in the scriptures could, at different times, occupy both positions and be a celebration of God *and* a warning of the wrath of God. Many books of the Bible relate accounts of the six-winged Seraph – a guardian of God – which was a fiery, furious creature. This creature could, on the one hand, instil terror in the ordinary people, demonstrating the power of God, or, on the other hand, be celebrated because of its majesty and beauty.

The "monster" of the Seraph stresses a key point here in that "monsters" have, throughout history, been read as symbols of a *variety* of different themes/issues/identities. In other words, there is no fixed meaning to the body of these creatures. They are some-thing which cultures create, in order to deal with their fears and anxieties, so that cultural phobias can be contained within the body of the "monster". In this respect, "monsters" are always subject to projection as culture transfers its anxieties onto this different body in order to deal with the terrors of the period.

However, while bodies such as the Seraph are mythical creatures, either symbolising the glory or the wrath of God, unusual human bodies were viewed in the same way. Indeed, Rosemarie Garland Thomson argues that all of our mythical "monsters" can be viewed as explanations for unusual or different bodies that have startled people from different cultures (1996: 1). Bodies that stray too far from what is considered to be the acceptable or predictable would be classed as "monsters" and explained by recourse to religious doctrine. Until the nineteenth century, it was common for surgeons to take the biblical examples as a precedent and diagnose "mon-strous" births as punishment from God (see Spinks 2005). Conjoined twins, for example, were either an omen of an angry God or, paradoxically, could be interpreted as something which celebrated the glory of God (see Shildrick 2002: 12).

By the seventeenth century, however, scientists started to seek scientific rather than mythical explanations for unusual or different bodies. However, they did not yet possess the scientific tools for investigation and so could only speculate on why differences were occurring. It wasn't until the early nineteenth century that teratology (the study of "monsters") was actually established within medical discourses. A greater understanding of the processes of reproduction and embryology allowed scientists to point out that unusual births were not the result of divine intervention but of atypical foetal development. A key figure in these debates was Professor Étienne Geoffroy Saint-Hilaire who published an influential thesis in 1822, arguing that "monstrous" births could be traced to unusual influences on the foetus while in development.

One of the key advancements made by teratology was that it changed the position of the "monster" from something unfathomable to something that was *almost* human. As a result of this, identification with "monstrous" bodies became possible and the same/other dichotomy, which had been in operation in narratives supported by myth, was broken down. It was from this period onwards that medical science began exhibiting unusual bodies – "monsters" – for the (supposed) purpose of education. These medical exhibits were intended to educate the people, informing them that "monstrous" births or unusual bodies were not the result of the wrath of God but of a variety of scientific factors that had contributed to unusual foetal development. (The next section considers how "freak" shows adopted this exhibition strategy from medical showcases but, unlike medical discourse, their agenda was entertainment rather than education.)

As a result of developments in scientific knowledge, the creature known as the "monster" exists now only in fiction. However, culture still maintains a burning curiosity about "monsters" and the fictional genre of horror continues to be one of the most widely consumed forms of entertainment. The continuing popularity of monstrous bodies probably comes from the way in which they function as 'magnets to which culture secures its anxieties, questions, and needs at any given moment' (Garland Thomson 1996: 2). There is no definitive meaning to a "monster" and it functions as a sponge, absorbing the anxieties of the time. For example, the ever-popular "monster" of the vampire has functioned in popular cinema as a metaphor for a variety of cultural anxieties. The vampire has been interpreted as a metaphor for anti-Semitism (*Nosferatu*), a metaphor for homosexuality (*Interview with the Vampire*, *The Hunger*) and more recently as an allegory for the pandemic of HIV/AIDS (the *Blade Trilogy*, *Ultraviolet*). Of late, the vampire seems to have been reduced to a metaphor for teenage moping and the "importance" of sexual abstinence (*Twilight*) but doubtless he/she will evolve into something different in the next decade. The point is that "monsters" function as a convenient metaphor, allowing spectators to believe they are actually considering topical issues while always being shielded from having to address these issues in too much explicit detail.

A key point about these representations is that they function as a convenient projection of our anxieties, allowing us to transfer our worries and concerns onto the mythical body of the "monster". Yet as Shildrick points out (2002: 19), the "monsters" which shiver our desires the most are the ones in which we recognise an element of ourselves – the creatures that inspire both a sense of difference but also similarity. Indeed, most "monster" movies will feature a sequence in which the hero(ine) exchanges a gaze with the "monster", acknowledging a sense of mutual recognition between the human self and the monstrous other. The "monster", in this respect, is often a symbol for the dark emotions which we cannot accept about ourselves such as lust or rage. Often this mutual exchange of gazes between "monster" and hero(ine) is coded in mirror-type iconography, suggesting the breakdown in the same/other dichotomy.

ENFREAKMENT

"Monsters" disappeared in the nineteenth century – lingering only as the characters of fiction. However, the unusual bodies, which had been identified as "monsters", were now labelled as "freaks". Garland Thomson points out that the word "freak" had originally meant a "fleck of colour" and then developed to mean whimsy or fancy. It was not until 1947 that the word became 'synonymous with human corporeal anomaly' (1996: 4). Indeed, the nineteenth century saw the fashion of the commercialisation of "monsters" in the performance spectacle known as the "freak" show. "Freak" shows became a popular form of "low" cultural entertainment, in both British and American culture, from the mid nineteeth to the mid twentieth century. Robert Bogdan (1988) argues that the genesis of the "freak" show can be traced back to 1850 when showman P. T. Barnum started exhibiting human curiosities in the American Museum in New York. Within a few years, this museum had attained unprecedented popularity and had set the template for what we now term as the "freak" show – soon to be thriving on both sides of the Atlantic.

One of the key points about the "freak" show was that it was a platform which turned unusual bodies into "freaks". This strategy of representation is known as enfreakment – a term coined by the critic David Hevey (1992). The thesis of enfreakment argues that the body may be different, strange, even unusual, but it is the mechanism of representation which renders this body a "freak". For example, in the "freak" show there would have been an exhibit, a human curiosity, identified as "The World's Fattest Lady". Undoubtedly this was a body which was very corpulent but it was the strategy of "freak" show representation which turned this corpulent body into "*The* World's *Fattest* Lady". She would have been exhibited on an under-sized stage in order to make her body appear so much bigger, she would have had padding under her clothes to increase her size and, of course, in the publicity blurb she would have gained quite a few pounds. Similarly, the exhibit known as "The Giant" would undoubtedly have been a man who was particularly tall but it was the strategy of representation in the "freak" show that would turn him into "The Giant". He would probably have worn a hat to increase the illusion of height, shoe lifts to add a couple of inches and, like "The World's Fattest Lady", would have been exhibited on an under-sized stage to promote the illusion of extreme height. In this respect, every person exhibited in the "freak" show was misrepresented to the public. Nobody is a "freak"; the identity of "freak" is a cultural construct created through discourses of representation (see Bogdan 1988: 10, 95, 267; Adams 2001).

Bogdan argues that there were two main modes of representation employed in exhibiting the "freak" to the general public: the exoticised mode and the aggrandised mode. In the exoticised mode 'showmen presented the exhibit so as to appeal to people's interest in the culturally strange, the primitive, the bestial, the exotic' (1988: 105). The spectators would peer at the exotic delight and marvel at the extraordinary quality of this exhibit's body. Underpinning a great deal of the "exotic mode" would have been a degree of eroticism and the spectators would have secretly delighted in the erotic frisson of gazing at the unbridled, animalistic sexuality of "the savage"; shivered with pleasure at the wiles of "the snake charmer" and undoubtedly savoured the sumptuous, creamy flesh displayed by "The World's Fattest Lady". Indeed, "The World's Fattest Lady" would have flaunted areas of her body which, for the period, would have been considered risqué and she may well have lifted her skirt up to give the spectators a glimpse of her magnificent thigh.

The other approach would have been the aggrandised mode of representation (Bogdan 1988: 188) in which the performing talent of the "freak" would have been emphasised. This strategy of representation would stress that the body was different – "freakish" – but was prodigiously gifted and an upstanding member of the community. Perhaps this unusual body had a beautiful singing voice or some other talent identified within the regimes of classical performance. Implicit in this mode was a particular politics of pity as the spectator would often be moved to tears by seeing how this unusual "freak" body was so gifted in a particular performance aesthetic and had not let his/her "freakishness" prevent him/her from performing.

Although official "freak" shows fell out of fashion in the mid twentieth century, various critics (Gamson 1998; Richardson 2010) have argued that these strategies linger on in contemporary popular media. Indeed, it might be fair to speculate that the "freak" show is back with a vengeance and now dominates popular television. Gamson has argued that many of our contemporary "chat shows" can be viewed as "freak" shows operating within the exotic mode of representation (1998). The spectators are allowed, under the guise of topical discussion/debate, to peer at the "freak" bodies for a short time. Similarly, the new craze for documentaries, in which a journalist meets an unusual body ("the woman with the largest breasts in the world", "the shortest man in the world"), can be read as operating as "freak" shows despite the programmes' claim to the contrary at the start of their narratives. Similarly, a number of "self-help programmes", which aim to show how the body *should* be managed and presented, can also be read as "freak" shows, especially in the way the unfortunate or unacceptable body is represented for public inspection. For example, is the British programme *Supersize vs Superskinny* a "self-help programme" that details medical reasons for maintaining a "correct" diet or a "freak" show giving the spectators the opportunity to marvel at unusually sized bodies?

Likewise, we can also trace a return of the aggrandised mode of representation – especially in our current fashion for talent shows. One body which was very much the object of this strategy of representation in her television debut was the singer Susan Boyle, whose audition on *Britain's Got Talent* became one of the most downloaded media clips in history. The programme initially represented Boyle as an object of ridicule – a foolish person to be laughed at. The editing showed audience members rolling their eyes and laughing at Boyle when she announced her ambition to be a professional singer. Similarly, the first backstage introduction of Boyle was accompanied by comedy music thus instructing the spectator that he/she was supposed to giggle at Boyle. The highly unflattering camera close-ups of Boyle in the backstage waiting area focused on her ungroomed hair, bushy eyebrows and unstylish attire (she was wearing white shoes with black tights).

Of course, the big shock was that an exquisitely trained singing voice could emanate from such an ill-managed body. The emotional response of watching Boyle's audition is very much the politics of pity mapped onto our own guilt. The spectator realises that one of the reasons Boyle may not have attained success was due to her unconventional appearance, which did not accord with contemporary culture's "beauty-ism", and then the spectator feels guilt for having judged Boyle in exactly the same way. Indeed, the emotional power of this audition cannot be overestimated and *Britain's Got Talent* has tried to reproduce the same effect in auditions in recent years.

However, the returning popularity of enfreakment strategies in popular entertainment raises the question as to why "freak" shows continue to be so popular. One of the most obvious answers is that we now live in an era which is obsessed with the management and discipline of the body (see chapter 3). As this book's first chapter has affirmed, we no longer think of the body as fixed or essential but as something which is shaped and transformed in relation to contemporary culture. As a result of this, people are anxious about the presentation of their own bodies. Am I too fat? Am I too thin? Am I muscular enough? How am I dressed? One of the pleasures of watching the representation of the "freak" body is that, arguably, it makes the spectators feel better about themselves. In other words, the "freak" body can function as a convenient defining other. Representations of "freak" bodies are ways of making the majority feel more secure by juxtaposing their well-managed, "appropriate" bodies against the defining other of the "freak" body. For example, a great many people nowadays are concerned about their weight – either that they are too fat or that they have gone too far with their diets and become too thin. A programme such as *Supersize vs Superskinny* represents extremes of weight – bodies that are classed as too fat set against bodies that are deemed too thin. Any of us who are anxious about our own weight can marvel at these extreme bodies on the screen and feel relieved that, irrespective of how fat or thin we may be, we're not comparable to the "freaks" on the show.

Indeed, from an historical perspective, this was the very reason why the "freak" show became so popular in the mid nineteenth century. This was a period of change in which communities were being fragmented and divided because of the move towards industrialisation and urbanisation. At times of social and economic crises, people want an affirmation that they are part of the accepted and established community – the fabric of society. The spectacle of the "freak" shows did just that by confirming a divide between the proper, working bodies of the spectators and the outsiders on the "freak" show stage.

Related to this idea of a proper, working social community is the development of the idea of the norm which, Lennard Davis argues, came into existence 1840–1860 (1995: 10). Although there have always been representations of the ideal human form (painting and statuary of ideal bodies have existed since the Greco-Roman empires), the concept of the ideal as something *attainable* for humans was not considered until the mid nineteenth century (see chapter 3). Prior to this, the ideal was the realm of the divine body and not the flawed, earthly body. However, as Davis points out, the ever-increasing need to account for people in terms of workforce statistics moved from simply being a way of documenting the State to a way of describing and quantifying average men and women (1995: 11–13). By formulating an idea of the average man and woman, based on his/her physical characteristics and potential contribution to the workforce, the idea of the required or well-managed body came into existence. As a result, the norm became linked to the ideal. No longer simply the dreams of artists and sculptors, the ideal body became the body that could contribute to the development of socio-economics. The "freak" show exhibit functioned as a very reassuring spectacle to the spectators in that it reminded them that they were part of the collective norm of society and not like those marginalised on the stage.

This, of course, raises the other key dynamic in enfreakment strategies in that the "freak" body can, like "monsters" before it, act as a sponge for all the anxieties of the period. In different contexts and cultures, different "freaks" have had greater popularity. In contemporary culture, we are now terrified of the, so-called, obesity epidemic (Monaghan 2008; Monaghan, Colls and Evans 2014; Rich, Monaghan and Aphramor 2011) and children are citing a terror of becoming fat as their greatest anxiety (see Bordo 1993). Therefore, the "freak" of "The World's Fattest Lady" becomes a convenient repository onto which we can map all our anxieties of the period. This exhibit is a convenient way in which we can contain all our fears and phobias about fatness in the one body of the "freak". This body is realising our fears, reifying them in the flesh, but, of course, is safely contained within the boundaries of the television show. We can be appalled, horrified, disgusted by "The World's Fattest Lady" (in whatever diet programme or documentary we're watching) but we can then turn the television off and forget all about it. In this respect, the "freak" body is still operating in a similar fashion to the idea of the "monster" as we considered in the last section.

However, there is a counter argument to this idea that the "freak" body safely contains culture's fears and provides a convenient, defining other for the well-managed bodies of the spectators. Various critics (Adams 2001; Gamson 1998; Richardson 2010; Stephens 2006) have reconsidered *how* exploitative enfreakment strategies *may* have been in the spectacle of the "freak" show or, indeed, continue to be in contemporary media "freak" shows. The image below (a publicity picture for Rita Cauda, a woman who made a career from being exhibited as "The World's Fattest Lady") demonstrates that the spectators are indeed using her as a defining other but yet there is also an ambivalent response to this "freak" body.

Image Courtesy of Münchner Stadtmuseum

The spectators' disgust and horror is quite clearly mixed with an erotic fascination for this extreme body. Cauda herself *appears* to be complicit in the enfreakment by lifting her dress to reveal her glorious thigh – thus absolving the spectator of any guilt in staring at her. (Whether Cauda really is complicit in the act of enfreakment would be open to debate. After all, this is her job and she needs to do this to make a living.)

However, what is happening here may be read as an inversion of the dynamics of beauty and spectatorship. Here we find a body that would usually be dismissed as ugly being the object of attention and fascination. Cauda's fat – usually a source of shame – here becomes a source of (erotic) allure. Therefore, it is *possible* to read the "freak" show (and contemporary strategies of enfreakment) not as an exploitation of unfortunate people but as a nuanced critique on culture's standards of what is deemed ideal and/or beautiful. As Robert Bogdan argues, 'during its prime the "freak" show was a place where human deviance was valuable, and in that sense valued' (1988: 268). Indeed, it would be possible to claim that one dynamic of the "freak" body is to force the spectator to reconsider his/her own politics of the normative. What is normative? What is beautiful? What is acceptable? What is proper? In that respect, it *could* be argued that "freak" shows were not necessarily exploitations of unusual people but a celebration of their extraordinary quality – a chance for these marginalised bodies to gain recognition, a voice and, in doing so, to challenge our preconceptions and prejudices about what is normative or acceptable (see Gamson 1998, Stephens 2006, Sweet 2001).

Most importantly, although "freak" bodies act as a defining other, there is also the element of recognition. The coding of the "freak" body always suggests difference but also similarity. As we can see in the above image of Rita Cauda, her size is a definite difference but yet she is dressed and styled in the fashion appropriate for a women going to a traditional ball or dinner dance. Given that fat phobia is contemporary culture's greatest anxiety, this image is unsettling in that it asks the spectator to consider if we really are all that different from this "freak" body.

Rosemarie Garland Thomson, on the other hand, cautions against a naïve celebration of the dynamic of enfreakment. Garland Thomson, one of the most respected critics within disability studies

(1996, 2002, 2009), argues that the "freak" show simply conflated all unusual or different bodies under the label of "freak" and therefore eradicated any particularity or specificity of difference (1996). Politically, is it correct to align the identity of "The Giant" – a body who is exceptionally tall – with the exhibit known as "The Frog Man" – a body who has unusually formed legs (which, arguably, resembled those of a frog) but who, most importantly, was unable to walk? In other words, one of the problems with excusing enfreakment narratives and representational strategies is that they did not acknowledge the identification which we now term disability. To return again to the example of Susan Boyle's first audition on *Britain's Got Talent* – an audition which was represented by the media in accordance with aggrandised enfreakment strategies – we realise that the one thing omitted from Boyle's introduction was the fact that this body is identified as disabled. Boyle has learning difficulties which often means that she struggles to find particular words in order to express herself. The audition, however, did not reveal this to the public but instead the spectators were simply shown a representation which appeared to be a foolish woman who couldn't even remember the word "village" when she was telling the judges where she lived. However, while the early "freak" shows predated the invention of the identity "disabled", Boyle's audition only happened a few years ago and therefore we should see it as frightening evidence that a new taste for enfreakment strategies is definitely returning to contemporary popular culture.

DISABILITY

The identification "disability" is itself a relatively young term. As the previous sections have outlined, bodies that were different and less-abled could only, until relatively recently, claim the identification of "monster" or "freak". The term disability replaced the labels "handicapped" and "crippled" – terms now considered inappropriate and/or offensive – in the 1970s. However, it has taken a long time for the term disability to enter into socio-legal discourse. For example, the Education for All Handicapped Children Act was established in 1975 and was only replaced with the more appropriate title Americans with Disability Act in the 1990s.

THE MEDICAL MODEL

Until the creation of a category of people identified as disabled, bodies which did not conform to the norm were – as the previous sections have outlined – branded either as "monsters" or "freaks". One of the key issues often overlooked in discussions of sideshow enfreakment – especially debates which question the exploitation of the "freak" shows – is that the exhibits were very often bodies who would now be identified as disabled. Indeed, the formation of a community of people identified as "crippled" was contemporary with the heyday of the Victorian "freak" show and, like it, was a response to the Industrial Revolution when there was a need to account for the workforce in the newly formed urban centres housing the massive factories. The Industrial Revolution of the 1800s saw the growth of new factories in the urban centres of the major cities and a need for bodies to work the machinery. Given that factory work required bodies to echo the speed and repetition of the machine, this work would largely have excluded people whose bodies did not conform to a particular standard. For example, if a particular type of factory work required the use of both hands, then a person missing an arm would be deemed inappropriate for this type of work. In short, factory work required a uniform workforce, in which bodies could work like automata, and was not designed to facilitate any form of physical difference (see Marks 1999: 80).

Another factor in the creation of the identity of disabled was the development in medical science of a branch which we now term biomedicine (see Foucault 1969). Biomedicine was concerned with diagnosing and classifying bodies that were different from the norm. From the Victorian period onwards, there developed an obsession in medical science with classifying and regimenting different types of bodies. For example, it was around this period that the invention of the sexually "perverse" – the homosexual – came into recognition. In previous times, people may have engaged in same-sex sexual acts but did not claim an identity from engaging in those acts (see Richardson 2009: 16–20). It was only because of developments in medical terminology that people engaging in same-sex sexual acts became identified as homosexuals. Similarly, biomedicine sought to diagnose and identify bodies which were deemed "flawed" and unable to contribute to the economic workforce.

In relation to disability, scholars identify this approach as the "medical model of disability". The medical model viewed disability in an essentialist light – in other words the bodies were "flawed" and unable to work. There was a medical "norm" established, identifying the "proper" body that could contribute to the workforce, and then there was the body who differed from this "norm" and was identified as "crippled" or "handicapped". If these "crippled" bodies could not be "fixed" or "repaired" then there was little use for them in the workforce and the best position they could occupy was that of victim or object of the politics of pity. The very best that a "handicapped" body could hope for was to inspire the pity and compassion of the able-bodied people and, indeed, a great deal of Victorian fiction represented the "crippled" child in order to inspire cathartic tears in the reader. The body of Tiny Tim in Dickens's *A Christmas Carol* is a fine example of the Victorian delight in this type of imagery.

A frightening aspect of the medical model, viewing disabled bodies in an essentialist light, is that this model could inspire fascist arguments asserting that there are "proper" bodies and then "improper" bodies – mistakes of nature. Of course, it's only a short jump from fascism to the even more terrifying eugenicist arguments which would assert that society should try to cleanse itself of "nature's mistakes" and encourage beliefs that these bodies should be destroyed at birth.

In summary, the problem with the medical model of disability is that it viewed disability in an essentialist light. The body was deemed "inappropriate" and "useless" simply because of its physical difference. If it couldn't conform to the work expectations of a particular environment then it was a "useless" body. It wasn't until the formation of the social model of disability that activists pointed out that the problem may not lie with the body itself but with the environment which did not make any allowance for this body's difference.

THE SOCIAL MODEL

The 1960s saw the birth of what Rosemarie Garland Thomson terms 'identity studies' (2002: 1). Based upon the theory of social constructionism, academic scholarship saw the rise of gender studies, sexuality studies, race & ethnicity studies and, most recently, disability studies.

If essentialism argues that an identity is innate, inherent in the person, and does not change according to culture or context, constructionism argues that identification (rather than identity) is premised upon the culture, era or context in which the person is located. In other words, a person's identification is the product of how culture reads the body's performances and presentations. To use an example of sexual identification, in contemporary Anglo-American culture we would identify two men engaging in same-sex sexual acts as gay. In Chicano culture, however, it is only the man who is passive during sexual activity who is identified as gay. The man who is active is identified as heterosexual (see Almaguer 1991). In other words, in Chicano culture sexual acts are identified in different ways from contemporary Anglo-American culture. In short, constructionism argues that there are indeed specific acts or performances but that how these are *interpreted* may vary from culture to culture. There is no inherent or specific meaning to be attributed to these acts; their identification is dependent upon how culture reads and labels these acts.

Constructionism underpins the social model of disability which draws a distinction between the physical impairment of the body and its identification as "disabled". The Union of the Physically Impaired Against Segregation (UPIAS) outlines the distinction as follows:

Impairment: lacking part or all of a limb, or having a defective limb, organism or mechanism of the body.

Disability: the disadvantages or restriction of activity caused by a contemporary social organisation which takes little or no account of people who have physical impairments, and thus excludes them from the mainstream of social activities.

(1976: 3–4)

In other words, "disability" is how society and culture respond to the body's impairment. As such, the identification of "disability" is socially constructed. The social model argues that disability is society's response to the body's impairment rather than viewing the disability as stemming from an innate or natural "flaw". Therefore, a body is only dis-abled if society fails to take any account of the body's physical impairment (see Barnes and Mercer 2003).

Let's take an example to illustrate this. A university professor has an impairment which means that he is unable to walk and so he uses a wheelchair. Within the context of the professor's job – in which his remit is to engage in scholarly research and disseminate the results through publication and teaching – the wheelchair may not make him any less able to do the job than someone who is not in a wheelchair. It would only dis-able the man if the university did not make any allowance for his wheelchair and did not provide wheelchair access to seminar rooms and lecture theatres. The point is that within the context of academic research, the professor's wheelchair would only be a disability if the university did not accommodate this difference and, say, asked him to lecture in a top-floor lecture theatre which did not have lift access. In other words, the "problem" would not lie with the wheelchair-using professor but with the university if it did not make accommodation for the professor's wheelchair. Therefore the social model would not view people with impairments as dis-abled or less-abled but as differently abled. People with an impairment would only be dis-abled if the context in which they were required to work did not make allowance for their physical difference.

Lennard Davis offers another excellent example which demonstrates that "disability" is a cultural identification by pointing out the difference that is maintained in contemporary culture between wearing spectacles and wearing a hearing aid (1995: 169). Specs and hearing aids are simply mechanical aids used to amplify a particular shortcoming: specs compensate for myopia (short sight) while a hearing aid assists some who has reduced hearing. However, the wearing of specs has now entered into fashion and many people are even buying clear glass specs (i.e. non-prescription) because they feel it enhances their particular "look". The same is not the case for hearing aids and, to the best of my knowledge, shops are not advertising "Designer Hearing Aids" intended to flatter a person's appearance. While both specs and hearing aids are simply mechanical aids, used to enhance a specific impairment, one has become fashionable while the other has not. This demonstrates that there is nothing fixed or innate about disability but it is simply a matter of how culture responds to particular impairments. Therefore, wearing a hearing aid will be identified as disability while wearing specs may well be interpreted as simple fashion – a person accessorising his/her look.

As can only be imagined, the social model has been a very welcome development for people involved in disability awareness and activism. As Tom Shakespeare points out, 'the achievement of the disability movement has been to break the link between our bodies and our social situation and to focus on the real cause of disability, i.e. discrimination and prejudice' (1992: 40). Yet despite this, the model has encountered some criticisms. One of the major criticisms is that the social model overlooks the specifics of the physical impairment itself. To cite the wheelchair-using professor again as an example, it is understandable to assert that the professor is only disabled if the university does not make allowance for his chair. However, what the social model is failing to acknowledge, in this example, is *why* the professor is using the wheelchair in the first place. Perhaps the professor has severe arthritis, so bad that it often makes him gasp and wince in pain. In this respect, the professor's arthritis may well interfere with his job remit as he may, on occasions, be in such pain that is un-able to engage in his research. The problem, of course, with acknowledging this issue is that it weakens the argument that disability is a social construct created by socio-cultural discourses which fail to take account of the body's impairment. As Tom Shakespeare points out, 'to admit pain, to confront our impairments has been to risk the oppressors seizing on evidence that disability is really about physical limitation after all' (1992: 40).

REPRESENTATIONS OF DISABILITY

The representation of disability in popular media is a particularly sensitive issue given that these images are unlike, say, representations of gender in that, for many spectators, there is no point of reference outside of the film text. For many spectators, their *only* experience of a particular form of disability may well be the depiction that they see on the screen. Therefore, the representation of a particular disability may well colour the spectators' perceptions as it is the only image to which they can relate. Even more worrying is that for disabled spectators, who may never have met anyone else with a comparable disability to themselves, the image on the screen is the only point of identification they may encounter.

As critics have pointed out (Zola 1985; Nelson 1994; Norden 1994; Wahl 1995) there were, and arguably still are, three main stereotypes of disability found in popular culture. The first is the evil disabled body: a person who has been driven mad or corrupt by his/her disability. This would include the tradition of evil hunchbacks ranging from Shakespeare's King Richard III to an assortment of cartoon villains in kids' entertainment.

On the other hand, there is the tradition of the sweet, young thing whose disability should inspire pity and compassion in the spectator. In our capitalist society, it is reassuring to find images that remind us that humans still have the potential for compassion and can take care of the "less fortunate". As cited already, the character of Tiny Tim in Dickens's *A Christmas Carol* is the prime example here. However, although these bodies remind us of our capacity for goodness they also serve to emphasise that we are fortunate enough *not* to be like them (see McGruer 2006: 9).

Finally, there is the tradition of saintly sages and blind prophets. These stereotypes are as old as Greco-Roman myth and are bodies which are often gifted with second sight or prophecy but are then dis-abled by literal blindness or some other physical impairment. In this respect, this type of representation very directly links disability back to the earliest ideas of "monsters" as symbols or the power and authority of God/gods.

Recent representations, however, have tried to revise and challenge these stereotypes. One very charming representation, which sought to address the very idea of dis-ability, was the British blockbuster *Four Weddings and a Funeral*. This film featured a deaf character, David, who was the brother of the leading character, Charles. David was not only an attractive character (he is described as a "dish" at least twice in the film) but someone who was represented not as dis-abled but as differently abled from the others. The film is remarkable for representing deafness as an asset within the film's narrative. It was only because of David's deafness that Charles had learned sign language and so, in one key sequence of the film, Charles is able to converse with his brother David in sign language when David is trying to convince him not to make a big mistake and marry someone whom he doesn't love. It is only because of the shared medium of sign language that these characters were able to converse across the spatial divide of the church. In this respect, deafness is not being represented as a dis-ability but a form of being differently abled and, in this context, a definite asset to communication.

The start of this chapter cited Rosemarie Garland Thomson who asserted that the different or extraordinary body was necessary as a means of self-definition for those who identify as normative. In recent years we have found an extreme variety of representations of unusual or different bodies in film and popular culture. While progress has been made in disability awareness, and some representations are addressing the issue with more sensitivity, we also seem to have returned to enfreakment strategies which not only fail to address disability with any degree of understanding but actually overlook the issue altogether. What is very clear is that culture's interest in the unusual body will not go away. While people in early Greco-Roman civilizations or early Christianity quivered in awe at the "monsters" of God/gods, we continue to marvel at the infinite variety of extraordinary bodies on our film and television screens and, either explicitly or implicitly, question our own position in the great regime of earthly bodies.

RECOMMENDED READING

MONSTROSITY

Shildrick, Margrit (2002) *Embodying the Monster: Encounters with the Vulnerable Self* (London: Sage)

A meticulously researched history of "monstrosity", *Embodying the Monster* offers a theoretically sophisticated analysis of these debates, drawing upon feminist cultural theory and phenomenology. Shildrick then develops the argument through many contemporary case studies such as the *Species* film series.

ENFREAKMENT

Adams, Rachel (2001) *Sideshow USA: Freaks and the American Cultural Imagination* (Chicago, IL: University of Chicago Press)

This text offers an excellent history of the "freak" show before then considering how the "freak" show has evolved since its "official" demise after World War II. Adams considers how the art photography of Diane Arbus and the fiction of Carson McCullers and Toni Morrison can be read as reviving the strategies of enfreakment. This book is very important reading alongside Richardson's text as its case studies are "high" art rather than popular culture.

Bogdan, Robert (1988) *Freak Show: Presenting Human Oddities for Amusement and Profit* (Chicago, IL: University of Chicago Press)

One of the most detailed examinations of the history of the "freak" show. Bogdan's text is still one of the most important books in clarifying the different modes of enfreakment: the aggrandised mode and the exotic mode. The final section moves the debates into a category which is more relevant to contemporary culture: the self-made "freak".

Garland Thomson, Rosemarie (ed.) (1996) *Freakery: Cultural Spectacles of the Extraordinary Body* (New York: New York University Press)

This is still one of the most important edited collections in scholarship on "freak" shows. Edited by an internationally respected scholar in these debates, *Freakery* is an extremely well-organised collection which guides the reader through the relevant debates. It not only introduces students to historical and theoretical case studies but updates this material through chapters which consider contemporary developments of the "freak" show.

Richardson, Niall (2010) *Transgressive Bodies: Representations in Film and Popular Culture* (Farnham: Ashgate)

This more recent book is an attempt to consider how the "freak" show spectacle has evolved throughout a range of contemporary, popular media including literature, pornography, film, television and the Internet. The book's argument is that culture creates the "freak" and then either contains the threat of this non-normative body or (s)exploits it within the particular text. This book addresses a range of "transgressive" bodies including transgender, fat, hyper-muscularity and disability. Although this text is intended as an academic monograph, it is written in a lively and accessible fashion which will be comprehensible for the novice student.

DISABILITY

Barnes, Colin and Mercer, Geoff (2003) *Disability* (Cambridge: Polity Press)

A short, introductory text written by two internationally respected scholars of disability. This text offers an excellent explanation of the social model of disability and is written in a lively, accessible style.

Davis, Lennard J. (1995) *Enforcing Normalcy: Disability, Deafness and the Body* (New York: Verso)

An extremely influential text within disability studies. Although the subject of the thesis is deafness, Davis's book has been much quoted in all fields of disability scholarship. The book contains many important insights into disability politics, awareness and activism.

Oliver, Michael (1990) *The Politics of Disablement* (Basingstoke: Macmillan)

A very important text in disability studies. This book is distinguished by its commitment to disability politics and is very much grounded in an awareness of the lived experience of these identifications.

BODY MODIFICATION

'The human body is so bland and unexciting. We cannot compete with the striking graphic dynamics of the zebra, the rococo flamboyance of the parrot, the hallucinogenic dazzle of a shoal of tropical fish or the subtle, textural variation of a leopard ... . Just as we possess no natural weapons or protective armour, so too must we resort to techniques of our own invention in order to be visually striking.'

(Polhemus and Marenko 2004)

This chapter considers how the body can be modified through practices such as tattooing, piercing and bodybuilding. As chapter 2 has explained, we all body-build via an assortment of body projects that we take on − "building" our bodies in order to conform to hegemonic standards. Chapter 3 considered the ways in which bodies are compelled by regimes of "beauty" so that many people modify their bodies to conform to hegemonic ideas. However, this chapter will consider bodies that attempt to oppose cultural hegemony and modify body image as an act of insurgence. We will explore these acts in more detail and consider the act of transgression, particularly with regards to *extreme* bodybuilding. Extreme bodybuilding, we suggest, offers up some intriguing ways into rebelling against the perceived cultural pressures on the body via extensive body modification. The first part of this chapter discusses some areas of, what is frequently termed, "skin art", which includes tattoos, piercings and other more extreme amendments to the flesh. The question we ask in this chapter is how transgressive is transgression (see chapter 2)? As we will demonstrate with the examination of bodybuilding, while traversing one line, the bodybuilder also positions him/herself within another (sub)culture in which the regulations of body image are even more restraining than hegemonic culture.

DEFINITIONS

The term body modification encompasses a wide range of alterations to the body. At one end of the spectrum, it concerns rather unremarkable and routine practices. For example, hair is one of the most readily amendable parts of the body. One could also include: eye make-up, painted nails, ear piercing, tattoos, shaving, waxing and tanning. Then there are modifications within the field of cosmetic surgery, for example: liposuction, Botox, facelifts, breast enlargement/reduction, rhinoplasty, abdominoplasty and genital surgery.

Mike Featherstone suggests that 'there has been a resurgence of interest in body modification in the West' and this covers a plethora of practices which include not only piercing and tattooing, as mentioned above, but also much more extreme alterations: 'branding, cutting, binding and inserting implants' (2000: 1). Falling under the same rubric, Featherstone adds bodybuilding, gymnastics, anorexia and fasting since, although the body is not altered using particular instruments, the 'outer body is transformed through a variety of exercises and dietary regimes' (1). Furthermore, he proposes that body modification incorporates 'various forms of prostheses and technological systems' (1) with the merging of human and machine producing the high-tech figure of the cyborg (as we discuss in chapter 6).

The term body modification encompasses a vast array of alterations to the human body which are beyond the scope of this chapter, but includes: genital beading, extraocular implants (otherwise known as eyeball jewellery), nipple splitting and removal, body suspension (where the body is hung from hooks), corset piercings (with piercings running up the back in two vertical columns), labiaplasty, male circumcision, penile subincision (splitting the top of the penis), eyeball tattooing and tongue splitting.

There are many individuals well known for having extreme levels of body modification, exemplified by Elaine Davidson (who holds the title of the most pierced woman in the world in the 2013 edition of *Guinness World Records*), Tom Leppard (the most tattooed senior citizen in the world) and Lucky Diamond Rich (who is the world's most tattooed individual with tattoos even on the inside of his foreskin, ears and mouth).

One can also see increasingly dramatic examples of body modification in Hollywood cinema. Numerous actors have gained substantial levels of media attention for radically changing their bodies to get into – or sometimes out of – shape for a role. For example, Christian Bale is often viewed as the ultimate "method actor" with his commitment to either bulking up for the Batman movies or drastically dieting down by more than sixty pounds for his role in *The Machinist* (2004).

Enid Schildkrout remarks that '[t]here is no known culture in which people do not paint, pierce, tattoo, reshape or simply adorn their bodies' (quoted in Plante 2007: 6). Outside of Western culture(s), there are copious examples of body modification, some of them extreme and, occasionally, disconcerting. For example, the Asmat tribe of West Papua, New Guinea, are remarkably distinctive with their noses pierced through with a pig's bone. Similarly, various Amazonian tribes pierce the lips with lip ornaments known as labrets. The Mayans offer another even more extreme example. As Lynn Vasco Foster writes:

> The head was artificially shaped in a process called trepanning, when the cranium was still malleable from birth. The baby's head was deformed into the desired shape by two boards tied to the head, one in the back, and the other against the forehead. Within a few days, the forehead was successfully flattened for a lifetime of beauty.

> (2002: 337)

What is evident is that contemporary Western body modification practices are very different from indigenous body projects, although they often borrow a number of styles and conventions. What also differentiates non-Western indigenous cultures from the West is the idea that we can transform our own bodies in a highly expressive and individualistic fashion. Anthony Giddens claims that since these changes in social roles were a product of late modernity (rather than postmodernity), they offer a 'reflexive project of the self'. According to Giddens, this means that 'the body is less and less an intrinsic "given", functioning outside the internally referential systems of modernity, but becomes itself reflexively mobilised' (1991: 7). This theme of the reflexive project of the self has been expanded upon considerably by many critics since. For instance, Susan Bordo (1999) defines the contemporary body as 'cultural plastic', in reference to the various ways in which bodies can be modified and manipulated through exercise, diet and also surgery. As such the body becomes the contemporary site of what is quite literally to be considered as *self-expression*.

Most recently, the role of modifications of the body which are transgressive has gained more critical attention (see Vale and Juno 1989; Featherstone 2000; Pitts 2003); and practices such as piercing, tattooing and branding have likewise been considered to be part of a self-reflexive attitude to the body.

TATTOOS

Today in Western culture(s) the most popular tattoos are Japanese themed, portraits, flowers and angels. Nevertheless, tattoos have a long history. Jane Caplan observes:

> Tattooing is one of many forms of irreversible body alteration, including scarification, cicatrisation, piercing and branding, and it is probably the oldest and most widespread of these. Physical evidence for the practice survives from the late fourth millennium BC in Europe and from about 2000 BC in Egypt, and tattooing can be found in virtually all parts of the world at some time.
>
> (2000: xi)

As Caplan suggests, tattooing has been practised by many different cultures for centuries and the reasoning behind tattoos has been varied. In ancient Japan, tattoos could be used for spiritual/religious reasons, or as markers of criminality (as in China too) (see Kuwahara 2005: 224); indeed, it is intriguing how tattoos have often been employed to signify outsiders. For some races, tattoos were used as a means of identification in the most appalling way, exemplified by Jewish prisoners in concentration camps during World War II.

The West was first introduced to tattooing during the 1700s when British sailors travelled to the South Pacific. As Alastair Couper explains, '[f]rom the time of Cook's arrival in 1769, foreign sailors underwent this ritual, possibly to show that they had been to the South Seas. Later it became a universal means of tribal identification as a sailor' (2009: 20). Like the fashion for piercings, tattoos have gained in popularity since the 1990s. Such an influence largely stems from celebrity culture, with a penchant for tattoos highly visible on the bodies of celebrities such as David Beckham, Angelina Jolie, Christina Aguilera, Tommy Lee, Megan Fox, Rihanna and, perhaps most surprisingly, Rupert Murdoch. And whereas tattoos used to be associated with working-class masculinity and, indeed, used by some working-class subcultures such as bikers to challenge the mainstream (see DeMello 2000: 138–139), there are now numerous professional people who have tattoos signifying a seismic cultural shift. Nevertheless, it should also be pointed out that between the late nineteenth and early twentieth centuries, tattoos also became desirable for the upper classes and some royals (see Shapiro 2010: 35).

PIERCING

The most pervasive form of body piercing is ear piercing which is replicated through many cultures and has a history that goes back thousands of years. Nipple and genital piercings have roots which go as far back as ancient Rome, although their appearance in the West is more recent. There is equally a long history of nostril piercing and piercings in other areas of the body such as the lip disc, with remarkable examples in Ethiopian tribes and several other countries. In his introduction to piercing, Housk Randall writes:

> Piercing – arguably one of the most widespread of the body arts among traditional peoples – had, until fairly recently, been regulated by Western society to the real of the outlaw biker and carnival sideshow performer. Aside from the notable exception of pierced earlobes for women, it was

certainly not an aesthetic possibility for the majority. Considered "bizarre", if considered at all, piercing became the focus of isolated sexual experimentation. Practiced by individuals whose imaginations seemed to have been inspired by the anthropological images printed in magazines such as *National Geographic*, it remained an almost completely unacknowledged activity.

(2002: 8)

In S/M communities and gay (sub)cultures, piercings have been popular for decades, yet it was the British take on punk that emerged in the mid 1970s which, as Randall remarks, 'truly brought piercing to the fore'. The aesthetic of 1970s British punk shared many similarities with that of earlier avant-garde art movements such as Situationism (and also Dada). The Situationists celebrated making art from the materials of everyday life. Punk had a very similar idea. Both punk and Situationism believed that the modern consumer was being alienated and hence needed to fight back. The means to do this was not just through punk lyrics, but by attitude and looks as well.

In his book *Lipstick Traces* (2001), Griel Marcus discusses the Situationist concept of *détournement*. *Détournement* for Marcus is the theft of aesthetic artefacts from their own contexts to be put into new contexts (167). This has much in common with sampling in pop music and with notions such as pastiche and parody, which are well-used terms in postmodern theory. The Situationists resituated their chosen artefacts in a disorienting fashion as a means of confronting society's stereotypes and biases. Punks used *détournement* in exactly the same way and this is clearly seen in punk fashion and style and, most noticeably, piercings. Safety pins, bin liners, toilet chains and the swastika were lifted from their original or familiar context and placed in a new setting. The punk's adoption of the safety pin represented an attempt to challenge and shock mainstream society, hence Dick Hebdige's perceptive description of punk style as 'sartorial swear words' (1979: 114). More recently, there has been a noticeable surge in tongue and lip piercings among youth culture which demonstrates the way in which piercings have – except for the case of more extreme examples (and here we are constantly having to reconfigure the term "extreme") – lost the ability to code such practices as deeply subversive (see chapter 2).

MORE RADICAL BODY MODIFICATION PRACTICES

What is clear with current body modification practices is that there is far more personalisation of such techniques than ever before. Rather than having some ritualistic significance, these practices reflect personal expression and, because of this, what is desirable for one person may not be for another. And as there emerge new technologies and medical techniques, so body modification practices have become more immoderate.

In Victoria Pitts's valuable study of various radical body modifiers in North America, she demonstrates how such an activity provides a variety of functions, most notably community building, social bonding, self-healing and cultural resistance (2003). In particular she focuses her attention on "modern primitives" who explore a variety of tribal body modification rituals from around the globe; hence, these people use such a framework when they tattoo, scar, pierce and brand their bodies. What's interesting is that many of the groups whom Pitts examines are white and fairly affluent. Pitts explores the way radical body modification has sometimes been used as a way to challenge the ordeal of illness. For example, when unwell, people may have to experience a number of medical procedures which, understandably, can make them feel out of control. Body modification is a potent way of regaining dominion of one's body. We want to briefly outline some of the more dedicated body modification practices before moving on to discuss bodybuilding.

Steve Hamworth is one of the founders of the Church of Body Modification and has been identified as the father of modern body modification. He is well known for designing specialist instruments to alter the body in radical ways such as ear shaping, tongue splitting and inserting magnetic implants. He states that the difference between plastic surgery and body modification is patent. As he comments: 'Plastic surgery is modifying the body towards what society considers normal. My art form is extreme individualism. Making you look more like everyone else is absolutely against everything that I do' (Grinding website). On their website, the Church of Body Modification outline their ideology with the following declaration:

> The Church of Body Modification represents a collection of members practicing ancient and modern body modification rites. We believe these

rites are essential to our spirituality. Practicing body modification and engaging in body manipulation rituals strengthen the bond between mind, body, and soul. By doing so, we ensure that we live as spiritually complete and healthy individuals.

(accessed 12 October 2013)

As Theresa M. Winge observes, the Church of Body Modification teaches the bond between mind, body and soul which enables a healthy space for 'spirituality and existence' and, she continues, the Church of Body Modification 'also indicates the Western search for Spirit in the ever mechanized and "mediated" body' (2012: 124).

Body hactivism, which emerged only recently at the beginning of the twenty-first century, was begun by a French photographer and artist Lukas Zpira. In 2004, Zpira produced a body hactivism manifesto that, unlike the modern primitives with their influence from tribal cultures, takes inspirations from science fiction cinema and literature, manga and comics. In many respects, Zpira's modifications upon himself, such as inserting chips and other implants under his skin, have echoes of the performance artist Stelarc, whom we discuss in chapter 6 with regard to cyborgs.

Earlier in the chapter we mentioned the popularity of Japanese motifs for tattoos and, indeed, Japan has a long history of this type of body art. Evidence of tattooing in Japan can be found in clay figurines dated 3000 BC or older that have painted marks that seem to represent tattoos. However, one of the most extreme present-day body modification practices is saline inflations and some of the more radical examples are to be found in Japan. In an article in the magazine *Bizarre*, which dedicates itself to all aspects of transgressive culture, the journalist Maki writes:

Picture the scene: five people, each with hideously distorted heads, tubes sticking into their faces. Reminiscent of a medical experiment gone hideously wrong, you'd be forgiven for thinking they had a gross infection or disease. They look like alien abductees, fresh from invasive research by their interplanetary masters. But these are Japanese club kids, otherwise known as bagelheads, deliberately disfiguring themselves by experimenting with saline inflations.

(2009: accessed 14 September 2013)

Although any part of the body can be inflated, this process is most commonly applied to the forehead with the injection of saline. The tissue becomes engorged and then malleable so that it can be sculpted into any particular shape. Such a pursuit in body radicalism follows on from other body modifications exemplified by scarification (cutting the skin) and implants (cutting the skin open and inserting an object inside). All of these developments on and to the body have echoes of modern primitivism which started in the 1970s in California. During the 1960s and 1970s, the West Coast was renowned for alternative religions, surfing, hippie subcultures and so on, all working against "mainstream" America. The main originator behind this movement is Fakir Musafar who declares that some people 'respond to primal urges to do "something" with their bodies' through, what he coins, 'body play'; this "play" also seems to imply S/M since his practice utilises pain endurance rituals (Klesse in Featherstone 2000: 15).

We now want to turn our attention to *extreme* bodybuilding, an activity which demonstrates some aspects of liberation through body modification yet intriguingly, also reveals the (male and female) body becoming hostage to the restraining codes of a subculture. (For further examination of the culture, practice and representation of bodybuilding see Locks and Richardson 2011.)

BODYBUILDING

> Discipline increases the force of the body (in economic terms of utility) and diminishes these same forces (in political terms of obedience). In short, it dissociates power from the body; on the one hand, it turns it into an "aptitude", a "capacity", which it seeks to increase; on the other hand it reverses the course of the energy, the power that might result from it, and turns it into a relation of strict subjection.
>
> (Foucault 1977: 138)

'You can take control of what you otherwise could not' claims "Andrew" who is not a bodybuilder but a "body modifier" who has altered his body through tattooing, scarification, branding, surgery, and body piercing (Pitts 2003: 1). In recent years such modifications to the body, and by extension the concept of the deviant or the "freak", have been recuperated by many in the West as a challenge to hegemonic definitions of the "normal". In effect, body modification lays claim to the body as the last remaining sovereign territory, one then literally inscribed as individual by virtue of markers like scars, tattoos, piercings, and so forth.

Writing on what unites the contemporary body modification movement, Victoria Pitts comments how its members:

> began identifying themselves and each other as "marked persons" or as body modifiers ... . Instead of an object of social control by patriarchy, medicine, or religion, the body should be seen, they argued, as a space for exploring identity, experiencing pleasure, and establishing bonds to others. A "deviantly" altered body was, as it had been in the past, also framed as a way to express social disaffection and rebellion and to establish one's membership in an alternative community, as well as to establish one's own individual, unique identity.
>
> (2003: 7–8)

In many respects bodybuilding echoes this definition. It is worth emphasising, at this point, that by "bodybuilding" we will be referring to competition-level bodybuilding. Although, as we have pointed out in chapter 1, it is true that we are all body-builders because we "build" our bodies on a daily basis, this section will focus on people who take the activity of building the voluntary muscles of the body to an extreme level. The top professional bodybuilding competitors today are those who possess the largest and most muscular bodies. Since prize money for top competitions such as Mr Olympia is offered only to the top six competitors – and with $650,000 awarded for first place – there is great impetus for a bodybuilder to produce as "freakish" a body as possible in order to win over the judges and crowd.

With the increasing popularity of aerobic, jogging and weight-training activities, pain is now an accepted part of the process of healthy exercise, but acquiring a bodybuilder's physique involves patterns of behaviour which move far beyond the realms of this new normality. Bodybuilding takes exercise and suffering to limits beyond *most* other sports, a condition signified by the all too apt descriptive terms for a bodybuilder's appearance – *ripped, sliced, diced and shredded* – terms which are indicative of far more transgressive reworking of pain (and again echoing other body modification subcultures such as modern primitivism).

The word asceticism originates from a Greek term meaning training for a particular goal or ideal (Yates 1991: 10). This objective can be sought for many reasons, though generally asceticism implies a denial of pleasure. Alayne Yates writes that asceticism has been historically linked to Christianity and can be seen through images of suffering, humiliation and death that circulate through Christian art (12). The ascetic monk exemplifies such a philosophy, discarding material goods and instead taking up a life of suffering, and Yates observes that the 'state of physical deprivation is a common factor between early Christian asceticism and the extremes of diet and exercise today' (12, 13). Yet there is a crucial difference between the two. Whereas religious asceticism involved goals that were directed to spiritual and non-worldly goals, athletic and dietary aestheticism directly involves the worldly self (13). The most significant example is weight training. In the last two centuries, attitudes towards exercise have evolved, but until the 1960s, weight training was believed to be detrimental to health because as a practice it specifically measured its utility in pain. However, from the 1970s onwards, and particularly with the increased popularity of aerobics, experiencing pain during (and after) exercise was seen as beneficial. The more the body hurt (the so-called "burn"), the more rewarding and efficient the exercise was considered to be. A professional bodybuilder appears to hold a perception of the body as an object that is both loved and loathed. Innumerable body-building magazine features suggest the body as some-*thing* to be battled against and overcome with titles such as: 'Blast Your Bi's', 'Armed for Battle', 'Full Blown Abs', 'Back Bombardment', 'Screaming Supersets' and 'Slice and Burn'.

Alan M. Klein writes how bodybuilding celebrates 'labour' by evoking the 'industrial imagery' associated with the phrase pumping iron, and indeed within bodybuilding magazines and websites there are numerous pictures of bodybuilders posed in the spaces of heavy industry (1993: 249). Klein remarks that in bodybuilding effort is fetishised by 'creating something that appears as both a by-product of labour and a precondition for labour: the muscled physique' (249). As Klein points out, Marx discussed the ideological implications of labour when he referred to commodities as not only the 'result of labour', but as also revealing 'the social character of men's labour'. This creates a form of alienation since the object produced is entwined in an economic system of production where 'everything is given exchange value' (249).

In the context of bodybuilding, it is the individual and the group (in competition) and the body and mind (in the self) which become estranged, generating a struggle between each (249). In order to build a large and defined physique, bodybuilders' routines are often represented as a battle between mind and body even when, and perhaps especially when, an injury occurs. One example appears in the most popular "hardcore" bodybuilding magazine, *Flex*, with regard to ex-Mr Olympia Dorian Yates (1992–1997) (*Flex* February 1995: 27–33). Written in the militaristic metaphors common to bodybuilding, signifying bravery and a fighting spirit, the narrative relates how Yates hurt his shoulder while performing a decline bench press – an injury which we are told was probably caused by overcompensating the left side of the body because of an earlier injury to his right triceps muscle. Meeting a specialist in New York, Yates was advised to have "corrective surgery" but refused 'because that would mean missing the Mr O with recuperation time' and instead he had cortisone injections as a temporary alternative (29). Then, nine weeks before his contest, Yates damaged one of his biceps. Even so, he still competed despite the severe pain he experienced in training and then in competition – and he won the title.

Obviously this article may be "bending" or exaggerating the truth slightly, in order to support the enfreakment fantasies common in the world of professional competitive bodybuilding (see Richardson 2011). Yet this commitment to the activity, and the staunch refusal to allow injury and pain stop the athlete from competing, echoes what Philip G. White, Kevin Young and William G. McTeer refer to as the process of 'reframing injury' in which an injury is repositioned as 'purposeful [and] appears to result from the machismo and fatalism of athletic culture, and from the persuasiveness of popular mythology about sport being a "character builder"' (White, Young and McTeer in Sabo and Gordon 1995: 176). In bodybuilding, this tendency is illustrated in the most extreme way since being injured and then still training is seen as typifying (in the context of the sport) an extra meritorious image of masculinity.

White, Young and McTeer note that other sports do prioritise pain over pleasure – otherwise known as the "pain principle" – but, as they state, only bodybuilders appear to 'convert pain into pleasure' (170). Where other athletes might deny, momentarily disregard or suppress being in pain, bodybuilders view regular pain in a more affirmative and open manner. This is most of all demonstrated in the core training of bodybuilding which involves repeatedly "repping" the muscle. The result produces the "pump", the moment at which the muscle engorges with blood and the pain of fatigue is replaced by a feeling of euphoria and pleasure. At its core, the process of bodybuilding is based upon the muscles being exercised to full capacity against weight resistance with each set being followed to the point of muscle fatigue and pain. Muscle cells are torn during exercise, causing pain, as does the subsequent soreness of the muscles after the pleasure felt by the "pump". In many respects bodybuilders believe pain to be an indicator that the exercise is working and thus their body is being shocked into growth. When this constant, painful process of injury through exercise becomes even too much for a bodybuilder and results in the forced cessation of training, many bodybuilders find this very difficult to accept. Writing of athletic injuries more generally White, Young and McTeer claim:

> Compromised health often confounds injured male athletes who are often dependent for their self-identity on physical power and fitness. Injury may involve, among other things, hospitalisation, missing competition, social dislocation from the team, even retirement. But equally stupefying for men used to silence around health care and negative bodily change are experiences such as unwanted weight gain or loss, feelings of ostracism, and depleted personal worth. In other words, athletes are forced to recognize, perhaps for the first time, that the physical body and its talents are integrally tied to self and to relationships. For men who conceive of sport in a principally gendered fashion, then injury has consequences for the *masculine* self.
>
> (1995: 171)

For bodybuilding, which relies so heavily upon the body to define the "masculine self", this is even more true and there often seems a reluctance to give in to the needs of the physical body. Such an attitude is at the core of the bodybuilder's mind/body relationship and there are innumerable examples of bodybuilders injuring themselves and refusing to stop training (as with the example of Yates noted previously), even (and sometimes especially) when physicians have told them that they must rest the injury. Klein recalls how in an early visit to a hardcore gym in California he saw 'a bodybuilder suffer a nosebleed while lifting weights; it was triumphantly explained [to Klein] that the man in question was a true bodybuilder, paying dues, training in earnest and willing to both risk and endure injury for his calling' (1993: 105). Klein also watched another bodybuilder 'doubled over in pain from what would later be diagnosed as a symptom of hepatic tumours on the liver and whose obviously unwell condition was again interpreted by the behemoths in the gym as testimony to his commitment to the subculture' (105). For Klein these men 'reinterpret signs of clear and present danger to their health as ringing endorsements of character' (105).

Klein clearly views bodybuilders as deviant, pathological and a danger to themselves (echoing many critics of body modification practices which, to them, signal pathologised or criminal behaviours; for example, see Favazza 2011). He observes:

> Sociologists have established a body of work that seeks to demonstrate how deviant behaviour is socially labelled, but also how deviant subgroups interpret this behaviour differently. Building on this view, social scientists using a cultural resistance model show how stigmatised groups view their behaviour. This perspective claims that, in response to being marginalized, these groups intentionally subvert the stigmas (behaviourally or as objects) assigned to them, and instead wear it as an emblem of status or resistance rather than shame.
>
> (1993: 105–106)

However, for Pitts, body modification practices, which often appear extreme and unsettling to those outside their subculture, need to be viewed outside of Western-based medical models in a celebration of the postmodern and post-essentialist body. The affirmation of pain in bodybuilding has similarities to other body modification practices. Referring to Paul Sweetman's discussion of tattooing, Pitts comments how such communities 'share an interest in producing new modes of embodiment that push the limits of normative aesthetics and often link pain and pleasure' (2003: 12).

An extreme example that compares powerfully in pain, dedication and presumably pleasure with bodybuilding is modern primitivism, a movement whose Western practitioners perform flesh hangings derived from Native American rituals in which the body is literally hung up by hooks through the flesh of the chest muscles. It is of activities such as this that Pitts writes:

> Not only is the postmodern body seen as an expression of an individual personality, but body projects are also seen in late/postmodernity as *integral* to the construction of the self, as Giddens argues ... . Following Giddens and Shilling, then, instead of revealing 'personality disorder and a propensity towards crime,' as the psychopathological and criminological theories would read them, body marking might be understood as a 'process of expression and reception' of meaning or a 'form of self-determination' within a postmodern cultural context. Body art has been seen as such a body project by a number of sociologists ... . Paul Sweetman, for instance, describes how body modifiers welcome the painful aspects of new body art practices as a way of exploring subjectivity ... . They gain, he suggests, a sense of accomplishment by enduring pain and healing the body. By expanding their sense of embodiness, they understand themselves as experiencing subjectivity 'to the full'. In this body–self relationship, body marking is used to create a 'coherent and viable sense of self-identity through attention to the body ... to anchor or stabilize one's sense of self-identity, in part through the establishment of a coherent personal narrative'.
>
> (2003: 31)

Thus it might be suggested that even though the bodybuilders Klein saw were clearly suffering, they were nevertheless performing their own body projects and writing self-narratives. Yet it is difficult to fully compare this with the subcultures of body modification, especially when knowing the damage to internal organs being inflicted through extreme bodybuilding. Paul Sweetman suggests that body modifiers gain a sense of well-being from not only the pain they cause, but also the curative process which follows (Pitts 2003: 31). However, as Klein documents, professional bodybuilding focuses on pain at the expense of recuperation. Intriguingly, the bodybuilder's determination not to stop weight training can best be correlated with Alayne Yates's analysis of individuals she names 'obligatory runners' (1991: 3). In interviews conducted with a selection of North American runners between 1983 and 1989, Yates states that a number of her subjects carried the sport to, what she describes as, 'unusual extremes' (3). Running had become the focus of their life's meaning; as 'obligatory runners', they continued to run when injured. Alayne Yates compares her 'obligatory runners' with 'eating disordered women' who she suggests show a range of similar characteristics (3). Both groups try to control the body through exercise and understand its relation to the burning up of calories (4).

The irony of bodybuilding, like the mandatory runner or the 'eating disordered woman', is that in the very act of trying to gain control over the body, the individual has – according to Yates – lost control. When bodybuilders are injured or are unable to train, they sometimes show similar withdrawal symptoms to Yates's groups, seeing their own body as deteriorating and suffering fluctuating emotions. The physique for the bodybuilder, as for compulsive runners and those with eating disorders, appears at times to be something seen as an object to be disowned or supplanted by a body that is stronger and more efficient. To quote Yates, the body is a territory that must be cherished, yet overcome, as a 'best friend and worst enemy', a phrase that seems equally applicable to some other extreme body modification practices (168).

The diet of a bodybuilder is another crucial factor in training to help create the winning (and consequently marketable) body. To enter a competition ripped and shredded, there needs to be extreme disciplining of the body through dieting. As the competition draws nearer, the bodybuilder begins a diet routine which does not seek to make the body healthier; instead the regime acts to unhealthily modify the body into an image that bodybuilders desire; yet, ironically, as the competition day approaches, the bodybuilder will feel weaker and slower.

It is most important to stress that this shredded look is a fleeting aesthetic, and can only be maintained for a few days at most. The top professionals even aim for a precise competition window in which they look their best, and the ultra-ripped appearance is so fleeting that a bodybuilder can appear more defined and vascular between prejudging and the main contest, even though both events are held on the same day.

Thus the irony of the sport is that although the outward look of the bodybuilder suggests health and strength, the dehydration and fat-reducing methods that reveal muscularity and vascularity actually weaken the bodybuilder's physical condition. Bodybuilding is one of a number of "high-risk" sports where the emphasis on weight control (either losing or maintaining), the stress placed upon the body, the emphasis on the individual over the collective and the need for leanness can lead to an eating disorder. Other sports include ballet, swimming, wrestling and gymnastics.

Although professional bodybuilding is widely acknowledged as unhealthy, its practitioners are still used to illustrate the top-selling magazines and supplements, supporting the notion that all levels of muscularity are healthy (when patently they are not). Nevertheless, the psychiatric condition known as "muscle dysmorphia" (also known as "bigorexia" or "reverse anorexia") suggests that some bodybuilders may be pathologically preoccupied with their appearance and believe that they are never sufficiently large or muscular (see Pope, Phillips and Olivardia 2000: 10–11).

We are cautious about a simple pathologisation which makes it easy to claim that the bodybuilder is suffering from a disorder of self-perception like anorexia. (It is also *highly* offensive to compare the masculine activity of bodybuilding with anorexia, given the history of how anorexia is implicated in regimes of feminine domination.) However, what is analogous to the illness of anorexia is the bodybuilder's extreme manipulation of his weight and refusal to listen (or at least respond) to the signals of his body. Thus the constructive paradox of professional bodybuilding is that bodily "perfection" can only come through ruination of the same body both through surface markings (as the result of drugs and exercise) and damage to the inner body (for example, the internal organs, and muscles and joints). As such, it represents an extremity – a "professionalisation", even – which other contemporary body modification practices do not resemble.

Branding, scarring, piercing, slashing and tattooing the skin leave permanent results and might also be seen to damage the body, but such efforts do not share bodybuilding's simultaneous effect on the body's internal anatomy. For example, steroids and growth hormone allegedly enlarge the heart muscles and other organs and damage the liver and kidneys, but patently tattooing and piercing do not. In this way, bodybuilding's relationship between the inner and outer body makes it not just far more transgressive and rebellious, but also far more problematic and resistant to narratives of recuperation.

Numerous academic texts on bodybuilding already pathologise bodybuilders because of their drug use. Others, conversely, make little mention of the use of drugs in the sport (see Dutton 1995), but it is apparent that many bodybuilders do have a detailed amateur knowledge of pharmaceuticals (see Monaghan 2001). Chemical assistance has become a component in all professional sport, but the bodybuilder, in a singular focus upon the body, would seem to be the most conspicuous and immoderate user of all.

Whereas until the early 1990s there was almost de facto censorship about steroid (and other drug) use in bodybuilding magazines and training guides, an abundance of information on ergogenics – legal and illegal – is now offered by bodybuilding magazines, textbooks and the Internet. The latter particularly now provides a staggering amount of material on how to self-medicate with illegal drugs such as steroids and growth hormone and also where to obtain these substances.

Inevitably, with the increase in size and definition in professional bodybuilding, greater combinations and stronger dosages of pharmaceuticals are required. In bodybuilding this is referred to as "cocktailing" in which a combination of drugs is taken to enhance the effect of another chemical or to suppress side effects of other substances. (For example, if the bodybuilder injects huge quantities of testosterone there is a risk that the body will convert this excess testosterone to oestrogen in a process called aromatisation. In order to combat aromatisation, the bodybuilder will need to use yet another drug called an aromatase inhibitor and these are usually prescription cancer drugs such as tamoxifen or, more recently, anastrozole and letrozole.)

Hence, the bodybuilder's usage of pharmaceuticals takes Western culture's obsession to "know your body" to extremes. Mark Simpson observed that bodybuilding was based upon 'the tyranny of the tape-measure: necks, calves, chests, arms, legs: the inches measure the man' (1992: 33). We would add that bodybuilding is equally, if not more, based on the tyranny of the dosage. With present bodybuilding, this numerical fixation is correspondingly directed towards the inner body. For instance, drugs are customarily measured in dosages of milligrams via injections or oral tablets.

Concurrently, food is weighed and demarcated through the percentage of carbohydrate-to-proteins-to-fat ratios. However, having an awareness of the consequences of one's body maintenance is less straightforward in relation to professional bodybuilding. The fact is that bodybuilders are now recorded as often taking enormous dosages of substances – the consequence of which cannot easily be known. This exemplifies one of bodybuilding's most "freakish" characteristics: its drive towards self-destruction, a subject often recounted in bodybuilding texts.

Clearly many other competition-level athletes use pharmaceuticals to aid their ability and there have been numerous reports of this – for example, in professional cycling with the recent scandal involving Lance Armstrong. Yet what singles bodybuilding out as more immoderate than other sports (and the mainstream more generally) seems to be not just its reliance on an ever wider array of chemical assistance, but also the use of pharmaceuticals which are not meant for human consumption at all. A case in point is the use of veterinary drugs. (Apparently, a recent powerful steroid – trenbolone – is intended for cattle.) Such extremities – if true – echo the tendency of contemporary body modification communities to signify the élan of their subculture with what are perceived from the outside as hardcore extremisms.

Many bodybuilders would claim that the bodybuilding community possesses the knowledge to safely self-prescribe, administer and monitor the use of drugs and other substances. Yet the growing evidence of side effects reveals a sport where the demand for physical excess makes the "safe" drug use seem problematic. For example, there has been considerable concern in contemporary bodybuilding that excessive use of growth hormone may cause a distended abdomen in the athletes either through the enlargement of internal organs or through an accumulation of internal, subdermal fat (see Hotten 2004). Many enthusiasts of bodybuilding have lamented that this "look" has ruined competitive-level bodybuilding and detracted from the "ideal" shape of broad shoulders tapering to a narrow waist. Similarly, in a subculture in which the use of anabolic steroids is all but mandatory, this increase in testosterone levels may result in greater quanities of oestrogen being produced in the body (unless a very strong aromatase inhibitor is used) and this may lead to testicular atrophy and depressed sperm production. A more visible side effect is gynecomastia – referred to as "bitch tits" within the subculture – where men develop soft breast-like tissue around the nipples.

However, it is not simply pharmaceutical side effects which can be seen to "queer" the bodybuilder's physique as there have been other writers and critics who have discussed the gender dissidence suggested by the extreme bodybuilder's physique. There has been an extensive amount of scholarship which has praised female bodybuilding for its challenge to essentialist ideas of feminine iconography, arguing that the female bodybuilder can be read as a feminist resistance to, or even an attempt to "queer", the gender binary (see Coles 1999; Kuhn 1997; Holmlund 1989; Richardson 2008; Schulze 1990).

However, there have also been a small number of critics who have argued that the *male* bodybuilder's physique presents a challenge to the normative regime of gender performativity (Dutton 1995; Fussell 1994; Richardson 2004; Shippert 2007). Sam Fussell, for example, notes that although the bodybuilder's physique, clothing and way of moving (referred to as the "walk") express allegiance to an intensely *masculine* subculture, there are aspects of this lifestyle which might be perceived as rather feminine rather than hypermasculine. Commenting upon the bodybuilder's gym bag as a 'tranny's handbag', Fussell writes how the competitive bodybuilder needs to carry 'Professional Posing Oil, Muscle Sheen, Pro-Tan Instant Competition Colour, sponge applicator tips, matte black competition briefs, and mousse' (1994: 42). He observes that, as such, male bodybuilding is 'less in the tradition of the circus strongman than the bearded lady. It's unnerving because it's so deeply androgynous. It's somehow simultaneously bully and sissy, butch and femme' (44). For Fussell, this gender dissidence gives bodybuilding a subversive potential, forcing the general culture to examine and question the conventions of gender. Other critics (Richardson 2004; Shippert 2007) have followed a similar argument and have argued that the extreme bodybuilder's body offers a haemorrhaging of semiotic meaning in the way that signifiers of masculinity are juxtaposed with semiotics of femininity. The male bodybuilder's physique is certainly angular and hard, reaffirming received signs of masculinity, yet this is also combined with curvaceous "plump" pecs, smooth, hairless, made-up skin and, in competition level, an abject level of vascularity (see Richardson 2004). As critics have noted (Creed 1992), the sense of the abject is inextricably linked to femininity. In this respect, there is a final irony: precisely as the bodybuilder becomes unacceptably "freakish" within his "freak" show, he becomes redeemable in terms of body modification sub-cultures, within which men and women have deliberately sought to blur, confuse, and surgically and chemically alter their genders, sometimes working deliberately towards an indeterminate "queer" status and image.

RECOMMENDED READING

Featherstone, Mike (ed.) (2000) *Body Modification* (London: Sage)

This is a valuable edited collection examining body modification practices such as tattooing, piercing, branding and implants. The book sets up the question of whether such practices suggest a return to a more tribal working upon the body, or whether it is more superficial than this. There are a plethora of informative articles by Featherstone and others, plus an insightful interview with the performance artist Sterlac upon the future of bodies in Western culture.

Locks, Adam and Richardson, Niall (eds) (2011) *Critical Readings in Bodybuilding* (London: Routledge)

Another edited collection which updates and addresses contemporary bodybuilding. This is the first collection to address the way contemporary bodybuilding has become increasingly more extreme and considers areas such as eroticism and sexuality that, up until now, have been largely neglected in academic debates. The study uses a range of different methodologies – qualitative and quantitative research, empirical and textual analysis – and is written by some of the key authors in this field such as Kenneth R. Dutton, Leslie Heywood and Joanna Frueh.

Pitts, Victoria (2003) *In the Flesh: The Cultural Politics of Body Modification* (New York: Palgrave Macmillan)

Pitts provides a fascinating examination of a range of body modifiers engaging in such practices as tattooing, piercing, flesh hangings and scarification. This important book is based on many interviews with participants in various body modification subcultures and is particularly interesting in that it looks at such alterations in relation to issues around the body, identity, sex and gender.

6

CYBORGS

'[T]he cyborg stands as a potent figure to help us think through our relationship with machines, and theirs with ours.'

(Bell and Kennedy 2002: 5)

In *The Postmodern Condition: A Report on Knowledge*, the French philosopher Jean-François Lyotard announces the emergence of postmodernism: 'Eclecticism is the degree zero of contemporary general culture: one listens to reggae, watches a western, eats McDonald's food for lunch and local cuisine for dinner, wears Paris perfume in Tokyo and "retro" clothes in Hong Kong' (1984: 76). First published in English in 1984, it has been quoted copiously and now seems rather obvious, even quaint. In the same year, the Canadian author William Gibson published his first novel entitled *Neuromancer*. The book will be dealt with at several points during this chapter (such is its importance), but suffice it to say here by way of a preface, it spearheaded a literary movement known as "cyberpunk" (see McCaffery 1994). Cyberpunk was fascinated with the relationship between man and primarily – though not exclusively – computer technology. Central to this enterprise is the figure of the cyborg, a being that blurs the boundaries between humans and machines. Advances in artificial intelligence, nanotechnology (of which more later), stem cell research and the Internet are just some of the examples of the cyborg's presence.

As Lyotard lists how people have become postmodern, so one might itemise the way they have transformed into cyborgs. At the more extreme end of the scale we have: cosmetic surgery, pacemakers, knee and hip replacements, deep brain stimulation implants (used for Parkinson sufferers), artificial legs and arms, eye implants, bionic ears (or cochlear implants) and artificial hearts. But there are a myriad of habitual technologies also employed: glasses, contact lenses, health supplements, mobile phones, iPods, computers and so forth. It has been suggested that dependence on mobile phones is so strong that, for some, suddenly not having this device can induce feelings analogous to the "phantom limb" syndrome experienced by amputees. Correspondingly, this powerful connection to gadgets is apparent in the way computers almost seem to read our minds. Amazon – and other online stores – suggests (often correctly) what we may want to purchase next. The collapse between inner self and the outside world has been discussed in post-structuralist thought by Derrida, Foucault and other thinkers, and seems increasingly applicable with the cyborg. This intensification between human/ machine, self/other, is equally indicated by a plethora of nascent devices on the commercial horizon such as augmented-reality glasses which offer wearable computer systems.

There is a vast array of literature on cyborgs in media and cultural studies, film studies, gaming theory, medicine, anthropology, science, art and a range of other discourses (for example, see Featherstone and Burrows 1995; Bell 2001; Bukatman 1993; Mason in Aaron 1999; Kirkup, Janes, Woodward and Hovenden 2000). Due to the complexity and breadth of the topic, this chapter can only provide a taster of the issues. For this particular section, we shall focus on analysing the cyborg in relation to physical bodies and online presence. We will offer a range of categories for defining the cyborg, and examine the cyborg as a concept that offers both worrying and optimistic visions for the future.

BECOMING BOND

For the most recent James Bond film, *Skyfall* (2012), the director, Sam Mendes, made a conscious decision to play down Bond's reliance on gadgetry. Traditionally, Bond has been given a variety of gadgets to equip him for missions. For example, there is a scene in the opening credit sequence of the Bond film *The Spy Who Loved Me* (1977) where we see the British agent making love to an unnamed woman in a log cabin somewhere in the Alps, but they are interrupted by a ticker-tape message which spools out of Bond's Seiko digital watch. The watch signifies stereotypes around British eccentricity in terms of inventors and inventions but, more importantly, suggests Bond is also like a machine, waiting to be activated by his boss, "M", when required. When he leaves the cabin and skies down the mountain, Bond's ski poles also function as guns. Gadgets are clearly a major part of Bond's identity. There is also a curious noise Bond makes when he somersaults through the air to evade his enemies' bullets. It's an unnatural, non-diegetic, electronic effect obviously not originating from Bond's fictional world, but has been added to heighten the experience of what the audience sees. This metallic-sounding sonic noise seems to connote that Bond is literally superhuman and machine-like in his abilities. Although twenty-first-century Bond is becoming more gadget-lite, the previous depictions of Bond's growing reliance on technology through the films shows the British spy becoming what we all are: cyborgs. To repeat, cyborg is a term to describe how people are becoming increasingly linked to gadgets and technology.

Although the average person doesn't have the more outlandish equipment loaned out to Bond such as car ejector seats and exploding pens, many people do have an increasing smorgasbord of gadgets. And even if we might not think we have many devices on our person, the increasing levels of convergence (where technologies merge with other technologies) indicate that, even with just smartphones, we now have a vast array of abilities literally at our fingertips. Because of the abundance of such technology in the present day, Sam Mendes considered their place in the Bond franchise as no longer exciting or special. The technocopia in the "real" world no longer warrants or requires such a fetishisation in the fantasy one of photochemical or digital film. The endless representation of futuristic and gadget-laden environments represented in 1960s television (exemplified by Gerry Anderson's puppet series *Thunderbirds* with its "rocket-porn") has, in certain respects, come to pass. And it is the increasing reliance on technology that makes the interface between human and machine progressively more evident.

To start with one particular example: the car. To drive a manual car (or "stick shift") involves a number of things: listening to the engine as it reaches a certain pitch before the need to change gear, paying attention to the rev counter on the dashboard, and constant use of the clutch pedal which alters speed and breaking capability. For the duration of that journey, both human and vehicle are working as one unit; human and machine become interfaced. Here the driver is an example of the cyborg as a category that blurs man/machine, human/non-human.

The influential Canadian theorist Marshall McLuhan remarks how the car, like many other technological inventions, is an extension of the human body, in this case the foot (1994). In a car we can travel quickly while being kept dry from the rain or cool from the heat. But McLuhan also views such "extensions" as the cause of "amputations". From the 1950s, American cities and towns were designed around the automobile while eradicating the need to walk. The car amputated the physical act of strolling which then affected people's health and the environment. (Similarly, various health problems have ensued from using other technologies. Many people suffer from "CVS" or Computer Vision Syndrome because of staring too long at computer screens. Likewise, headphones – especially earbud headphones which sit inside the ear – can cause hearing loss. Both technologies offer extensions in terms of the eye and ear, yet at the same time produce amputations.) This plays into concerns with an over-reliance on technology causing humanity's subsequent downfall, which is a key theme of dystopian narratives popularised in cinema and television as we will explore later in this chapter. Such fears are also covered in literature, most (porno)graphically in J. G. Ballard's novel *Crash* (1973). Here the interface between human and machine is taken to its violent conclusion and the car becomes an extension of not only the human body, but the act of sex itself.

To continue the car analogy, a driver will sometimes comment how they often have no conscious recollection of the minutiae of detail en route. Driving without conscious thought has been referred to as "zombie behaviour" (see Koch and Crick 2001). One is so familiar with driving that the act becomes an example of a biological–mechanical interface. Operating a car encourages a symbiotic relationship that allows the driver to partially "switch off". They become one with their car/machine.

Much technology, particularly because of its increasing ease of use – exemplified by the iPad – is encouraging a partial "switching off", which further supports arguments that people are becoming closer to their machines. Indeed, one of the earliest definitions of a cyborg is technology used 'automatically and unconsciously' (Clynes and Kline in Gray, Figueroa-Sarriera and Mentor 1995: 31) – something that more user-friendly technology increasingly allows. When watching children confidently using computers, there is a noticeable speed and ease with which they operate these systems; there seems to be a "natural" interface between them and the technology. Their familiarity seemingly requires less conscious engagement, rather like skilled pianists who reach a level of expertise that enables them to play without conscious influence. It is often remarked how children are far more at ease with technology than older generations and therefore appear more connected to machines. In light of this, it may seem that children are the more obvious examples of cyborgs although, as will be emphasised in this chapter, we are all cyborgs now.

Although there is literature to suggest the contrary, we suggest that cyborgs are not to be confused with androids and robots. Cyborgs are human and machine, whereas androids and robots are completely artificial. To make this distinction clearer, we want to set out some definitions of these two other categories before working through the concept of the cyborg.

ANDROIDS

The term "android" began to gain use in science fiction in the 1940s. Android means "man-like" and was originally used to describe automata. Unlike robots, androids look human. They are organic copies of humans. In literature, early depictions of the android can be seen in Mary Shelley's *Frankenstein* (1818) where the creature is assembled from the body parts of cadavers. In H. G. Wells's *The Island of Doctor Moreau* (1896), Moreau's bio-anthropological research transforms animals into mutant hybrids.

Unlike robots, androids in science fiction are especially troubling as they so closely resemble the human image. This takes us into theories of the postmodern simulacrum as set out by the French philosopher Jean Baudrillard. According to Baudrillard, in the postmodern world, simulation heralds a period where images have taken over from reality. We live at a time where images have no relation to reality, yet they seem preferable to reality, for example, the images/ signs of advertising. For Baudrillard, it is now the age of simulation where there are copies of copies of copies ad infinitum. Reality has been so saturated by images, reality itself has been fundamentally changed. Baudrillard also refers to this as hyperreality which Steve Best and Douglas Kellner see in two different ways: 'weak' and 'strong' (Best and Kellner 1997: 103). 'Weak' hyperreality is where people can see a clear difference between real and simulation. For example, if I visit Disneyland, I can see that it is a simulation of the real; yet for some people, it is far better than the real world. In contrast, 'strong' hyperreality is where people cannot tell the differ- ence between the simulation and the real. Baudrillard gives the example of the rest of America outside Disneyland which hides the fact that it isn't real either (1983: 25). As Richard J. Lane explains:

> [Baudrillard] ... calls Disneyland ' ... a deterrence machine set up in order to rejuvenate in reverse the fiction of the real'. What he means by this is that Disneyland exists to convince us that rationality is outside the walls of its childish domain, rather than the fact that rationality has been replaced by childishness everywhere.
>
> (2000: 90)

Scott Bukatman suggests that simulation/hyperreality is applicable to reading the android. As he writes upon the replicants (or androids) in *Blade Runner*: 'Jean Baudrillard's discourse on simulation ... the copy had superseded and even surpassed the original. Map replaced territory. The only important difference between humans and replicants was programmed: a four-year lifespan operates as a fail-safe mechanism, protecting the human form from its own obsolescence' (1997: 65).

Androids are also a further example of 'strong' hyperreality. These are duplicates of humans who cannot easily be distinguished from their flesh-and-blood masters. In *Westworld*, there is a scene near the end of the film where the main character escapes from a hazardous robot-gunslinger and discovers a woman imprisoned in a dungeon pleading for water. As she drinks, she starts to break down, exposing her as another robot. As Adam Roberts observes: 'It is impossible to tell human and machine apart' (2006: 117). But with androids, any such reveal is more challenging.

In *Blade Runner*, the human lead, Deckard (played by Harrison Ford), detects replicants by the use of a "Voight-Kampff" test which identifies non-humans through an empathy-testing procedure. *Blade Runner* places a great deal of attention upon the philosophical question of memory in relation to being human (the replicants collect photos to quell this lack) and, in relation to this, real and faked emotions. We never know how real the replicants' own emotions are. The Voight-Kampff test is designed to trip them up on this very "fault". Yet such a lack might also be directed to us. One might ask, are emotions such as anger or joy only experienced because we live in a culture which teaches us such things? If so, could not anger and joy be programmed into non-human life? Although androids are copies of humans, the film asks the tricky question of whether these beings have emotions, a consciousness and even a soul. At the end of *Blade Runner*, the leader of the replicants – Roy Batty – dies. At the moment of his death, a dove flies symbolically up into the air. This is a curious scene that, on one reading, makes some kind of signification of a soul/life force exiting the android's body. Such questions problematise the notion of what it is to be human and how this might be *replicated*, hence illustrating one reason why the android generates such anxiety in fiction.

ROBOTS

Robots are made out of non-organic materials; in other words, they are machine-driven. If one looks at the kinds of robots which work for us doing precision tasks in factories (such as making vehicles), we can see that they are programmed and, thus, controlled. Early versions of mechanical entities were called automata, but in 1920 a Czech playwright called Karel Čapek wrote a play entitled *R.U.R.: Rossum's Universal Robots* introducing the term "robot". While the robots in *R.U.R.* are essentially androids as they are organic, the term has stuck and refers to forced labour. In Čapek's story, the robots are exploited factory workers who eventually rebel and overpower humanity. The etymology of the word "robot" is interesting as robots are slaves. There are various ethical problems of robots as slaves since, once these machines gain greater levels of intelligence, it would, perhaps, encourage a desire for autonomy and freedom. *Blade Runner* (1982) addresses such problems as we will see shortly.

There are also robots such as Hal 9000 from *2001: A Space Odyssey* (1968), Johnny 5 from *Short Circuit* (1986), *The Iron Giant* (1999), *WALL-E* (2008) and C-3PO and R2-D2 from the *Star Wars* franchise. Most are slaves/servants and this is made apparent through the films' narratives, yet they have an obvious quality of humanness. For example, WALL-E is lonely, not a characteristic one would associate with a machine. Similarly, C-3PO acts like a neurotic English butler, while R2-D2 behaves like a toddler emphasised through its beeps and whistles which signify it as an infant, albeit through an ARP synthesizer. Similarly, the robots (or drones as they're referred to in the film) in *Silent Running* (1972) are clearly an influence for R2-D2 with their personalities and child-like charm.

From the 1920s, numerous pulp magazines such as *Amazing Stories* were published catering for an interest in science fiction. In these publications, robots were seen as malevolent machines intent on terrorising mankind. During the 1930s, often termed the golden age of pulp science fiction, science fiction clearly marked out two threats to humanity: inventions of war and machines that could think for themselves. In pulp fiction these robots were represented as crazed electro-mechanical monsters.

The robot signalled that very bad things happen in science fiction and this was hardly technology leading to progress. Many cinematic examples can be cited throughout the decades, most notably *Westworld* (1973) which parodies consumerism with its robot "entertainers" running amok at a Disney-esque holiday resort. Nevertheless, it was the writer Isaac Asimov who championed a new breed of robot who could actually help mankind.

Before Asimov, there had already been a few robots which were promoting a friendlier image to the public. For example, Elektro was a seven-foot robot exhibited at the 1939 New York World's Fair and whose humanity was suggested by his witty replies to audiences and his ability – most apt for the time – to smoke cigarettes. Unlike fictional narratives in film and literature, Elektro was clearly a robot under human subjugation. Asimov's robots were also under human control as created in his Three Laws of Robotics taken from his short story 'Runaround' (1942). As outlined in his Three Laws, robots would benefit mankind and this directive would be upheld because of their programming. As has been widely noted, these laws have 'passed into received sf scripture' (Jones in James and Mendlesohn 2003: 167). Such ideas are illustrated in the film *Forbidden Planet* (1956), featuring one of the most iconic robots in cinema: Robby the Robot. Because of people's misgivings with machines due to a steady diet of dystopian science fiction narratives, it is initially hard to trust Robby, especially since he is the creation of a stereotypically obsessive scientist Dr Morbius. Yet in one particular scene, Asimov's laws are clearly demonstrated when Robby is instructed to shoot a human; he cannot and commences to short circuit. The central theme that emerges from *Forbidden Planet* is that machines are far more principled than their human creators.

CYBORG

The term cyborg (from "cybernetic organism") was introduced by neuroscientist–inventor Manfred Clynes and psychiatrist Nathan Kline in their 1960 article 'Cyborgs in Space' (see Clynes and Kline in Gray, Figueroa-Sarriera and Mentor 1995: 29–33). The 1960s was the time of the Space Race between the United States and the former Soviet Union. In their paper, they write about 'adapting man's body to any environment he may choose' (29). 'Space travel', they suggest, 'challenges mankind not only technologically, but also spiritually, in that it invites man to take an active part in his own biological evolution' (29). As Andy Clark remarks: 'Why not, in short, reengineer the humans to fit the stars?' (2003: 170).

The cyborg concerns a human having technological enhancements. In reality, this could be anything from bionic limbs or an artificial heart to a microchip in the brain (for example, giving complete fluency in a language without the need for learning). With the idea of a human having any part of the body replaced/enhanced by machine components, a cyborg future points to a time when any part of the body can be substituted. Although the central nervous system and the brain are the only two parts of the body which cannot be replaced (yet), the notion that everything else in one's body has an artificial reserve suggests that cyborgism points to a time when death may be overcome. Marvin Minsky, who is a leading figure in the field of artificial intelligence, is one of the more outspoken advocates of this cyborg future, which he sees as an antidote to our dissatisfying evolvement from an animal that has a very short life span. Such a yearning is also reflected in Transhumanism: an intellectual movement that sees technology radically lengthening human life expectancy.

While the idea of having body parts replaced as they wear out is a fact of life for many people – for example, knee and hip replacements have become routine – the degree of enhancement to which Minsky refers still lingers in the discourse of science fiction. Nevertheless, even at these less spectacular levels, such day-to-day operations are examples of people becoming cyborgs. For the cyborg anthropologist Amber Case, our status as cyborgs is equally marked by the technology external to us. As she observes: 'You're cyborgs every time you look at a computer screen or use one of your cell phone devices' (2010). We will return to this observation a little later.

We now want to examine a number of different types of cyborg. We suggest that there are three main categories for understanding this concept, which we will discuss in turn: the physical cyborg, the virtual cyborg and the cyborg which is a mix of both physical and virtual.

PHYSICAL CYBORG

This is the most familiar image of the cyborg as part man, part machine. One of the best known representations of the physical cyborg is from the television series *The Six Million Dollar Man* (1973–1978). Based on the novel *Cyborg* (1972) by Martin Caiden, the series focuses on an astronaut who is seriously injured while flying a NASA research aircraft. (The opening footage of the crash was taken from a real accident in 1967. Miraculously the pilot survived, but suffered permanent health problems unlike his fictional counterpart.) Austin becomes the world's first bionic man with bionic legs (enabling him to run at speeds of 60 mph), a bionic arm (giving him superhuman strength) and a telescopic eye. Cinema and television offer plenty of examples of the physical cyborg, including

Darth Vader, Inspector Gadget, Iron Man and RoboCop. In sport, a prominent example of this category of cyborg is the South African sprinter and double amputee, Oscar Pistorius, whose legs have been replaced with J-shaped carbon fibre prostheses designed to replicate the curve of a cheetah's leg. There is a long history of prosthetics dating as far back as the ancient Egyptians with one mummy having been buried with a prosthetic toe, although it is in the twentieth century that significant advances start to be made with, for example, the first pacemakers coming onto the market in the 1950s.

CYBORG AS VIRTUAL BODY

With this category, the body is discarded – or at least temporary left behind – as one enters into cyberspace. In William Gibson's novel *Neuromancer*, he envisages a world where people "plug in" to a computer via a jack at the back of the head. In Gibson's narrative, the body is referred to as "meat", which, given the characters' pleasure in living out virtual existences over "reality", implies a loathing of flesh. Roger Luckhurst explains:

> Case begins the novel unable to jack in, his nervous system sabotaged by merciless employers: 'For Case, who'd lived for the bodily exultation of cyberspace, it was the Fall ... . The body was meat. Case fell into the prison of his own flesh'. Flesh is weak, and, for many feminist critics, nearly always encoded as feminine in cyberpunk ... . Molly's body experiences all the pain and suffering cyberspace can evade, and her past as 'meat puppet' (or prostitute) further emphasizes the fallen nature of the body.
>
> (2005: 208)

The virtual body is often presented as the vanguard of social change in its receptivity to technology which promises to transcend the human form. Cyberspace spectacularly offers a way of escaping from the confines of our bodies and the environments we inhabit. The self becomes vaporous and fluid. Relevant here is embodiment theory. This concept presents the idea that a sense of self is contingent on the physical body. At a time where images of "perfect" bodies abound in the visual media, embodiment has become strongly linked to notions of a successful and attractive self. Feminists such as

Simone de Beauvoir write how women are enslaved by bodies which menstruate and become pregnant (see Boynton and Malin 2005: 208–209). Similarly, in *Neuromancer*, Case perceives his body as a prison to be escaped and cyberspace offers the allure of disembodiment. There are numerous films where a virtual, disembodied existence is seen as preferable – and in numerous ways, superior – to corporeal existence, for example: *Tron* (1982), *The Lawnmower Man* (1992) and *The Matrix* (1999). We will consider virtual cyborgs – and *The Matrix* – in more detail later in the chapter.

A MIXTURE OF BOTH PHYSICAL AND VIRTUAL CYBORG

The cyborg presents a future where we can have more and more replaceable body parts – legs, arms, eyes, hearts and so forth. In the 1950s the term "built-in obsolescence" was coined to describe the way manufacturers made products built to last for only a limited amount of time so consumers would need to buy replacements. Ageing is programmed into our genes, so we too have a kind of built-in obsolescence. However, the cyborg offers a solution to the problems of wear and tear and the inevitability of death.

One such solution might be where human consciousness can be downloaded to another body (or medium), which is an idea vividly illustrated in Hans Moravec's *Mind Children* (1988). In the novel *Neuromancer*, Case has a brief moment living through Molly which gives him a highly erotic sense of being transgender. Such an experience (sometimes referred to as cybersex) is where there is an opportunity for playing out different sexual identities. A microchip implanted into the brain might, one day, offer opportunities for people to live out others' experiences. This raises several philosophical questions such as the relevance of your "original" body (and the concept of gender) and the possibility that, if consciousness could be copied into something else, it could also be copied multiple times; hence, one could create multiple copies of the same person. With scientific discussion considering the possibility of one day being able to download an individual's personality into a chip – or even being able to download experiences directly onto the Internet – the organic body could be left behind. Cinema has provided some intriguing depictions of living out another's experiences through virtual technologies, most notably *Brainstorm* (1983) and *Strange Days* (1995).

More recently, James Cameron's *Avatar* (2009) depicts a paraplegic marine who downloads his mind into a cloned body of an alien. Following on from *Avatar*, there have been reports in the media of experiments in Switzerland with an individual who is partially tetraplegic. Allegedly, the test subject has been able to move a robot by using just his brain signals; it is a long way off Cameron's vision, but does afford a preview of a future where the mind controls other "bodies".

FEARS AND POSSIBILITIES: CYBORG AND THE POSTHUMAN

The cyborg offers a startling new moment for the evolution of mankind which has been termed in some quarters as "posthuman". Ihab Hassan discusses posthumanism as far back as 1977, writing:

> We need to understand that the human form – including human desire and all its external representations – may be changing radically, and thus must be re-visioned. We need to understand that five hundred years of humanism may be coming to an end, as humanism transforms itself into something that we must helplessly call posthumanism.
>
> (1977: 212)

There are many useful texts upon the posthuman, in particular Martin Heidegger who, in his 1955 essay 'Questions Concerning Technology', expresses a common concern that technology will take us over. The fear of humans becoming cyborgs is that technology starts to take away our control of things, and such trepidation is expressed by Heidegger and many others since (see Fukuyama 2002). For example, implanting chips into the human brain to allow people to surf the net without having to manipulate a keyboard is just one of the many areas being explored by scientists. Yet such a future also leads to worries about the mind and body being taken over by some exterior force (i.e. governments).

At present, the American military is using neuroscientists to develop insect-cyborgs. Initially these were going to be tiny flying robots fitted with surveillance technology, but then scientists realised the benefits of using living insects which could then be enhanced (or cyborgised). As Emily Anthes remarks: 'All they'd have to do was figure out how to hack into the insects' bodies and control their movements' (2013: 20). Scientists eventually found a suitable specimen – the flower beetle – in which they made tiny holes into the brain and into the muscles that power the wings. Fixed to the beetle's back was a backpack with various bits of electronic equipment to send signals to its brain. Manipulating rats' brains through neuroscience has being going on for many years (and takes us all the way back to the origins of the cyborg with Clynes and Kline who also experimented on rodents), but Anthes points to an opportunity for members of the public to have a go at "biohacking". She notes:

> In 2009, Gage and Marzullo established Backyard Brains, a company that sells low-cost kits that will turn any interested amateur into a neuroscientist ... . For their second product, Gage and Marzullo decided to push the boundaries further, to venture beyond brain observation into brain control. Taking inspiration from the world of cyborg animals, they created a kit that provides their customers with all the tools they need to take over the nervous system of a living cockroach ... . If you're new to the hobby of animal mind manipulation, the cockroach is an excellent place to start. Because a roach relies on its long, fluid-filled antennae for a host of sensory and navigational functions, its nervous system is stunningly easy to hack; all a wannabee roachmaster has to do is thread a wire inside each antenna. ('It's like it's designed to be a cyborg', Marzullo says.)
>
> (2013: 21)

Anthes points to a (very near) future where children will be able to hack into animal/insect brains for pleasure. Yet, such fears are also directed at the possibility of mind manipulation of humans. Mind control has always been a popular staple of science fiction narratives, most famously depicted in Aldous Huxley's *Brave New World* (1931), although here it is control through drugs. There are countless books and articles detailing state experiments by countries throughout the decades; the CIA were particularly keen to experiment with LSD in the 1960s as a means to reprogramme and control human behaviour. Brain/mind chips seem to touch a nerve, both figuratively and physically, with the image of involuntary cyborgs, i.e. people becoming cyborgs against their will on a permanent basis. For many years computers have been seen as threatening to take over our lives and eradicate free will, and this is taken to its nightmarish conclusion with (microchip) mind control. We will return to this idea when we discuss dystopian cyborgs in television drama. But first we want to briefly consider Donna Haraway who is one of the most prominent figures debating cyborgs. For Haraway, the cyborg offers a very exciting future – although it is one she sees as also unavoidable whether we like it or not – with far-reaching consequences for gender relations in a posthuman age.

During the period of modernity, it is suggested that individuals were more fixed down by a sense of self. In our period of postmodernity, which began in the late twentieth century, identities have become noticeably more fluid and mutable because of a number of factors such as television, advertising and fashion. This is also manifest in the way we deal with others through various electronic communication systems. In cyberspace there is the idea that people can escape from their body, play with other identities and, most radically, become postgendered. Feminist theorists such as Claudia Springer, Sadie Plant and, most crucially, Donna Haraway have discussed such ideas.

In 1985 Haraway wrote an influential essay entitled 'A Cyborg Manifesto'. 'By the late twentieth century,' she writes, 'we are all chimeras, theorized and fabricated hybrids of machine and organism; in short we are cyborgs' (1991: 150). Haraway's cyborg manifesto (as with much of what she has written since) is not for the faint hearted and it is often a taxing read for undergraduates. Yet Haraway offers a valuable text which has had a seismic impact in the fields of technology and science studies. Haraway remarks that even though the cyborg is 'the illegitimate offspring of militarism and patriarchal capitalism', she points out that 'illegitimate offspring are often exceedingly unfaithful to their origins' (151). Furthermore, Haraway's concept of the cyborg works against 'seductions to organic wholeness' (150). For Haraway, the cyborg inhabits a postgender landscape that moves away from notions of essentialism and the restrictions of a patriarchal society. For many years, Haraway has seen cyborgs as offering a breathtaking future for feminism fused with technology. She shares a similar engagement with other feminist theorists such as Judith Butler who challenge essentialist gender positions. The notion that technology – particularly virtual environments – allows the body to start to dissolve, fragment and disperse resonates with the (equally opaque) books by Gilles Deleuze and Felix Guattari who also celebrate, what they term, 'a body without organs' (2004: 9). Nonetheless, while Haraway's work is indispensable for debating the possibilities of postgender – and for making the notable point that technology isn't just for men – representations of cyberculture in more popular media still appear largely male dominated. This is exemplified by the covers of many computer/gadget/gaming magazines and science fiction fantasy art with depictions of hysterically muscled men and busty women, both of which work against Haraway's resistance to wholeness and static notions of gender. The cyborg as posthuman is most darkly represented in images from cinema and television, and we now address examples from the latter.

SPACE NAZIS

Like cinema, television has offered up some nightmarish visions of cyborgs and we shall consider two of these: Daleks and Cybermen.

DALEKS

In the long-running British science fiction series *Doctor Who* (1963–1989, 2005–), the Daleks have been the show's most popular enemy of the titular time-travelling hero. Daleks are a mutated race from the planet Skaro who live inside a mobile casing equipped with sensor discs, a sucker-stick arm, a long stalk with iris and a laser gun. The natural form of a Dalek is a green, blob-like octopod with claws. Because they are a clear crossbreed of biological creature and machine, they are cyborgs. The sole *raison d'être* of a Dalek is to "exterminate" all other life forms. The Daleks feature in many episodes of 1960s *Doctor Who*, but by the 1970s they are clearly symbolising the Nazis with their endless quest to wipe out other races and advocating genetic purity (see Sleight 2012: 106). Their harsh electronically processed voices add to a creature which has absolutely no redeeming qualities whatsoever. They fulfil a popular fear of the cyborg: a thing without pity. James Chapman points out the irony that a creature so hideously amoral should be adored by children who watch the show, but that probably comes down to the Dalek's iconic design (2006: 29). Even so, the Daleks as cyborg nightmare play into two particular fears: fear of nuclear war (which has mutated the creatures – the "Kaleds" – resulting in their encasement within a Dalek shell) and fear of technology erasing any shred of morality. Chapman writes: 'The Daleks represent an extreme form of technocracy: they live in an ant-like colony with a structured, hierarchal order, they are entirely rational and they have lost all conscience or sense of morality' (28). The observation that Daleks live out an insect-like existence is noteworthy as this is a shared image with the Doctor's other "monster" rivals: the Cybermen.

CYBERMEN

The Cybermen have been another regular foe in *Doctor Who* since the 1960s. The Cybermen originate from Earth's twin planet, Mondas, and, so we are told, the Mondasian civilization developed far more quickly than Earth's. The Mondasians evolved into ruthless creatures where logic replaced emotions and organs were replaced by cybernetic parts giving way to the birth of the Cyberman. Cybermen have achieved the Transhumanist goal of immortality; their only weakness is gold which destroys their breathing apparatuses. The Cybermen are much stronger than humans, but their endless quest for physical augmentation has left them utterly dehumanised with no emotions. In a story entitled 'The Tenth Planet' (1966), a Cyberman explains that '[o]ur brains are just like yours, except that certain weaknesses have been removed ... . You call them emotions, do you not?' It is the voice of the Cybermen which is particularly haunting: mechanical like the Daleks, but with no emotion (the Daleks are characteristically angry cyborgs often shouting at each other and their enemies). The first appearance of the Cybermen is especially disturbing since they never move their lips when speaking; the words come out as if pre-recorded, and then the mouth shuts again. Their faces are covered with a surgical stocking which points to the horrors of radical surgical amendment. In the story 'The Tomb of the Cybermen' (1967), their first appearance is marked by insectoid imagery as they break out of tomb-like casings as a swarming mass. Like with the Daleks, cyborgism robs these cyber-people of any individuality and their mantra is: "You will be assimilated"; in other words, eradicate difference. There are echoes here of films such as *Colossus: The Forbin Project* (1970) where machines are emotionless, arrogant and practically omnipotent. As the series continues, the Cybermen appear increasingly mechanised; for example, organic parts (mainly jaws) can occasionally be glimpsed, but eventually the entire body becomes metal. The only exception is the cyberleader whose human brain is revealed under Perspex casing in his/its helmet. The Cybermen are a palpable example of science fiction playing into areas of body horror (see Sleight 2012: 58).

NANOTECHNOLOGY

First discussed in 1959 by physicist Richard Feynman, nano-technology promises to be the ultimate technology which could have a profound impact on the body. Rebecca L. Johnson defines nanotechnology thus:

> Nanotechnology is a new scientific field that involves moving individual atoms and molecules around to create new things on an ultra-small scale. Some of these things are never-seen-before materials with remarkable properties. Others are tiny 'machines' – smaller than microscopic viruses – that can do specific jobs. Nanotechnology is a whole new way of building things … . Almost every manufactured thing you see – tables, computers, shoes, books – have been made from pre-exisiting materials such as wood, stone, cotton, metal, leather and plastic. These materials have been cut, shaped, ground down, woven and formed into these objects. Nanotechnology works the other way around. It doesn't start with big things and whittle them down. It builds things from the bottom up, atom by atom, molecule by molecule. The arrangement of atoms and molecules in a substance determines its characteristics. So it makes sense that rearranging those atoms and molecules will change the substance's characteristics. If you could do that, you could also control – very precisely – the characteristics of whatever you were making. That, in a nutshell, is a big part of what Nanotechnology is all about.
>
> (2008: 6, 8–9)

In *Star Trek: The Next Generation*, the crew of the *Enterprise* starship have a machine known as a replicator which reassembles molecules of an object to create a totally different thing; with regard to *Star Trek*, the replicator is primarily used for making food from recycled waste. The premise behind this is nanotechnology. If nanotechnology can allow anyone the chance to be able to recreate anything by transforming atoms, suddenly the very basis of capitalism would be under threat. At present, nanotechnology is still in its infancy (although the use of nanoparticles is now evident in sports equipment, health-care and clothing); however, it signals the beginning of a revolution for controlling the physical world.

One of the areas being developed is nanobots. These are machines made out of atoms. The goal of such devices would be to perform particular tasks such as mending cells, repairing tissues and destroy-ing cancer cells. Nanotechnology might also be used to grow new organs which would herald the death of the cyborg since the cyborg, by its very definition, is a mix of person and machine. In the age of nanotechnology, the Six Million Dollar Man's broken legs would be re-engineered while remaining organic; there would be no need for bionics. Nanobots could perform this re-engineering without the need for machinery to be added to the body.

Yet as with many nascent technologies, there are fears that nano-technology could just as equally be a significant threat to the body. For example, there are discussions around nano-sized devices that could be implanted into the brain to control behaviour (a fear shared by notions of the cyborg as we saw earlier); other fears include nanobots being used by both the military and, in response, terrorist organisations. As one account speculates:

> By attacking certain kinds of metals, rubbers and lubricants of conventional weapons, specifically designed nanobots could destroy these weapons by consuming them. When bionabots [i.e. nanobots] are ingested from the air by a person, they could assay his DNA codes, release specific gene drugs and self-destruct in the body.
>
> (Varadan, Pillai, Mukherji, Dwivedi, Chen 2010: 22)

In our current period that is witnessing such technological accel-eration, nanotechnology takes the trend of miniaturisation to its extreme and offers a future where the body can be extraordinarily enhanced and chillingly ravaged. As one of the key figures in nano-technology – K. Eric Drexler – comments, nanotechnology offers 'engines of creation' and 'engines of destruction' (1996: 171–190).

CYBORGS AND VIRTUAL IDENTITIES

Earlier in the chapter we cited the author William Gibson who coined the concept of "cyberspace". As Gill Branston and Roy Stafford suggest, cyberspace 'offered a new world in which human experience was "digitised" and interaction took place in the "virtual reality" of datastreams' (2003: 438). Although we have not yet reached the level of immersion represented in Gibson's narratives, there are some noteworthy examples of how far technology has come along. For example, Second Life is an online 3D world where people select an avatar – which is their on-screen self/persona – to then interact with other avatars in an astonishingly involved virtual world that even has its own currency. In Second Life, it is often unclear if the persons behind avatars are the same sex or age – often they are not. As Susie Orbach writes: 'The absence of embodiment does strange things to people. It dematerializes their existence and enables the fashioning of new identities in the postmodern age. There is no need to be limited by the physical, the actual, the person one has been up to now' (2009: 79). Orbach also remarks how a virtual existence creates "hazards". She notes:

> The immediacy of email and internet communication produces unexpected emotional entanglements. Like the teenager who falls for the bobble-hatted ski instructor on the slopes, only to recoil from the vaguely familiar balding forty-year old man leering at her on the dance floor several hours later, it is easy for us to project on to a cyberspace companion intense longings and desires and a sense of being understood and responded to that we haven't felt before.
>
> (78)

While Second Life is at the more extreme end of the self becoming virtualised, there are plenty of other examples of how we now have digital doubles made of bytes and bits. Having a Facebook profile and a Twitter account are just two examples of what Amber Case calls our "second selves". She explains:

> Whether you like it or not, you're starting to show up online, and people are interacting with your second self when you're not there. And so you have to be careful about leaving your front lawn open, which is basically your Facebook wall so that people don't write on it in the middle on the

night because it's very much the equivalent. And suddenly we have to start to maintain our second self. You have to present yourself in digital life in a similar way that you would in your analog life.

(2010)

These "second selves" also play into ideas around surveillance. The surveillance technologies we have today are getting more pervasive, but these also extend to data-veillance. Each of us leaves a trail of digital information as we move physically through the urban landscape, coupled with visual recognition technologies, searchable databases and so on. But we all have digital personas now whether we like it or not, echoing our earlier reference to Haraway who said changing into a cyborg was inevitable. We might have set these up with our Facebook accounts, but these "second selves" can also be more insidious. The way you shop, your shopping habits, your viewing habits online: these all impart valuable commercial information. These "second selves" (or as they are also called, "data-doubles") become your online subjectivity. They might not be recognised by you, but might actually affect your life in significant ways. How many times do you check your credit rating? Maybe you don't need to yet, but at some point you may find that you can't get a loan and, if you go and check your credit profile, you might find how your "second self" has impacted on your "real" self. What happens if this information is about you having some life-threatening disease? You might unexpectedly discover that you can't get insurance. All of a sudden you may not be employable anymore because, according to this online information, you could die in a couple of years, so your company might not want to invest in you. Therefore, one's "second self" can dramatically affect life beyond the virtual, demonstrating the overlap between human and digital selves.

Gaming is another example of where online identities can become amalgamated. Various studies have offered some interesting perspectives upon players' identities and their bodies. In a series of physical and psychological tests on computer gamers to see whether game playing could be considered a sport, one researcher suggests that the gamers react almost as quickly to visual stimuli as fighter jet pilots, yet their fitness levels are poor (*Telegraph* online 2010). The top gamer of the study allegedly has the physical fitness of a heavy smoker in his sixties.

The idea of humans enhancing their mental agility while their bodies atrophy is a common narrative in early science fiction exemplified by the British science fiction writer H. G. Wells. In an essay entitled 'The Man of the Year Million' (1893), Wells comments how the future might produce humans with large brains and emaciated bodies: 'their whole muscular system, their legs, their abdomens [will shrink] to nothing, a dangling degraded pendant to their minds' (2009: 85). The hostile aliens in Wells's novel *The War of the Worlds* are horrific glimpses of a race which prioritise mind over body; as he writes, 'they are heads – merely heads' (2008: 112). Although the sedentary lifestyles of (some) gamers may be making them unfit, extreme disembodiment is still only the preserve of film. In the Wachowski brothers film *The Matrix* (1999), the film sets out the question of whether cyberspace – otherwise referred to as the Matrix – can give rise to a far superior type of (post)human. In the narrative, the main character of Neo (played by Keanu Reeves) finds out that his life is simply an illusion which has been created by hostile machines. Jim Baggott explains:

> In reality, his body is trapped in a capsule of viscous pink nutrient. A cable feeds electrical signals to the base of his skull, and thence to his brain. Everything he has ever experienced in his life has been a virtual reality simulation called the matrix, fed to his mind by a belligerent machine intelligence which, though originally created by humans, has now turned on them and is using human bodies as sources of energy. The matrix is used to keep passive the minds and hence the bodies of virtually the entire human race.
>
> (2005: 8)

Neo is a cyborg in that he has tubes plugged into his body, yet this isn't an empowering vision of the cyborg; he is being used by machines as a human battery. *The Matrix* is indebted to William Gibson's novel *Neuromancer* in numerous ways, but particularly so regarding fears of technology – i.e. computers – getting too powerful, resulting in their eventual control of the world. Douglas Kellner comments how the move from the modern to postmodern is a movement from where technology is 'an extension of human beings, who use technology to control and dominate nature' to where now 'technology is taking over and is in control of humans who fight for their freedom, their power, their autonomy, their humanity' (1995: 308). (There is already evidence of such fears with, for example, a report by the Human Rights Watch, dramatically entitled 'Losing Humanity: The Case Against Killer Robots' (2012). The report flags up worries with key nation states developing autonomous robot weapon systems which may pose a serious threat to humans.) This is certainly the situation for Neo who faces a machine-led genocide against humanity.

Neo has echoes of the German philosopher Friedrich Nietzsche, who wrote upon the emergence of an "Overman" (or *Übermensch*), a difficult and often confusing term, but one loosely referring to what Dave Robinson calls those who 'strive to go beyond human nature' (1999: 30). Daniel O'Brien reads the contemporary Overman as concerned with the 'enhancement of the human species [using] technology, the modern Ariel, to aid him' (2000: 39). In the matrix, Neo is a verifiable superman who literally does fly off into the sky at the end of the film. His body in the "real" world is far frailer, which is further emphasised by the way he is penetrated by wiring. Yet when the film concludes Cynthia Freeland observes, '[t]he perfect, exciting, memorable Keanu/Neo is intact, closed up, with no openings or flaws, no vulnerability – in short, with no relationship to his actual physical flesh-and-blood body' (2002: 209). It is intriguing that the film concludes with this image of Neo: powerful, godly and, perhaps, transcending the human (body). The film doesn't provide any clear message about the self-inhabiting cyberspace/the matrix, but does imply that we live in a world where the media has created a new form of subjectivity which is 'saturated with information, images and events' and where the media no longer reflects reality, but creates it (Sarup 1996: 112).

CONCLUSION

For some cultural commentators, the label cyborg seems too extreme a label for the average person. This might seem fair enough when looking at individuals such as the Australian performance artist Stelarc who has worn prosthetic limbs, had an ear surgically implanted onto his arm and – because of his cyborg identities – often refers to himself as "we". One could also point to Professor Kevin Warwick who has had numerous implants inserted under his skin in a desire to become the "world's first cyborg". Similarly, Rob Spence is personally involved with experiments with various camera-eyes to replace an eye which was lost in an accident. And there is Neil Harbisson who operates a device that lets him actually hear colours to compensate for his colour blindness. Such examples take us into the realm of body modification and new forms of identity construction which we discuss in chapter 5. Most of us have not gone that far into cyborgism, but as we have argued in this chapter, it is a definition by degrees and, therefore, even on a more modest scale, it is a label which seems ever more applicable. To be a cyborg involves utilising some bodily technology from the seemingly mundane (for example, wearing glasses/contact lenses, having a filling, taking vitamin tablets or listening to music on headphones) to the more extreme (plastic surgery and prosthetic technologies). From such a broad spectrum, it would seem humans have become a hybrid and such technologies are replacing the organic. In his essay 'Cybernetic Organism', Isaac Asimov writes:

> We can imagine, little by little, this part and that part of the human being replaced by inorganic materials and engineering devices. Is there any part which we would find difficult to replace, even in imagination? I don't think anyone would hesitate there. Replace every part of the human being but one – the limbs, the heart, the liver, the skeleton, and so on – and the product would remain human. It would be a human being with artificial parts, but it would be a human being. But what about the brain? Surely, if there is one thing that makes us human it is the brain ... . It is the brain, then, that is the sticking point in going from human organism to robot.
>
> (1987)

Our essential humanness is a difficult thing to define because human development and social interaction have always been contingent on enhancements – be that through the use of an axe during the prehistoric period, or our mobile phones today. For Asimov, substituting bits of our organic selves as they break down doesn't stop us from being human – the authenticity of being human always remains if there is a brain. Yet as we have seen in this chapter, even the brain is viewed as an organ that is desired – and predicted – by some to be eventually transgressed and replaced.

With the ever-competitive climate of gadgets, numerous technology industries are now working on wearable appliances (see Seymour 2010). What is palpable is how the body has now become a major focus for new devices. For example, appliances have recently been designed to not only provide information based on one's location, exemplified by augmented-reality glasses mentioned in the introduction, but also monitor a heartbeat and prewarn against strokes. The Cyberman mantra – "You will be assimilated" – seems a prophetic battle cry as humans become increasingly symbiotic with their machines.

RECOMMENDED READING

Bell, David (2001) *An Introduction to Cybercultures* (London: Routledge)

This is an extremely useful introduction to cybercultures which fleshes out some key concepts, such as cyberspace, with clarity and insight. There is also a helpful glossary at the end of the book.

Bukatman, Scott (1993) *Terminal Identity: The Virtual Subject in Postmodern Science Fiction* (Durham, NC: Duke University Press)

An absorbing book whose title points to the eradication of the human and the birth of a new virtual subject. Writing from the perspective of cultural studies, Bukatman examines human identity in relation to the Information Age and utilises a wide range of theorists such as Jean Baudrillard and Donna Haraway.

Featherstone, Mike and Burrows, Roger (1995) *Cyberspace/Cyberbodies/Cyberpunk* (London: Sage)

A very accessible edited collection looking into the effects of technology upon the body. The introduction is particularly useful for unpacking the various key concepts discussed throughout the book.

Gibson, William (1984) *Neuromancer* (New York: Ace)

A hugely influential novel which was one of the first texts to coin the term "cyberspace" and powerfully depicts a world becoming obsessed and modified through cyber-technologies.

Haraway, Donna J. (2004) *The Haraway Reader* (New York: Routledge)

Haraway is one of the most significant voices discussing cyberculture, especially with regard to her pioneering work on the notion of the cyborg. This is an excellent selection of her work and includes her 'Manifesto for Cyborgs' and more recent work on the study of animals.

Hayles, Catherine (1999) *How We Became Post-human* (Chicago and London: University of Chicago Press)

A very interesting book that explores the idea of embodiment in our technological age and examines the concept of the cyborg and the birth of the posthuman.

Kirkup, Gill; Janes, Linda; Woodward, Kath and Hovenden, Fiona (2000) *The Gendered Cyborg: A Reader* (London: Routledge)

Using Donna Haraway's 'Manifesto for Cyborgs' as a starting point, this fascinating edited collection examines representations of the cyborg in a number of areas such as science fiction cinema, the Internet and discourses around reproductive technology.

GLOSSARY

Adonis complex An ambiguous, and highly contentious, term which describes a man who is concerned about his level of physical attractiveness and wishes to make himself more desirable. The term comes from the character in classical mythology – Adonis – who was revered for his youth and beauty. Some critics use the term "Adonis complex" as a synonym for "muscle dysmorphia" in which the subject feels he is not muscular enough. However, these terms can only be viewed as synonymous if we understand muscularity as being the *only* feature of masculine beauty. Another related term often used is "bigorexia" – an inversion of anorexia – in which the subject feels he is skinny and puny and desires to be as extremely muscular as possible. However, "bigorexia" should also not be confused with the "Adonis complex" as the bigorexic subject desires to become hypermuscular while aware that this may not accord with dominant ideas of male attractiveness.

Body image This term refers to a person's perception about the level of attractiveness of his/her own body. Although the term has been in use for several decades, in more recent times critics have used it in relation to the influence exerted by the contemporary media in shaping people's ideas about how their bodies should look.

Body modification A term that refers to someone who deliberately modifies his/her physical appearance. It is usually presumed that such a term refers to the more extreme end of body modification such as tattooing, scarification or transdermal implants. Nevertheless, it could be argued that we all engage in some kind of body modification with, for example, the cutting and/or removal of hair.

Bricolage A term used to describe the putting together of a new stylistic assemblage by re-using and re-purposing existing artefacts. Youth subcultures are one example of bricolage in the way that they appropriate artefacts from more mainstream culture and change their meanings. The most dramatic example of this is punk during the 1970s which used seemingly disparate elements such as safety pins, bin liners, toilet chains and, especially, the swastika for clothing. These items were lifted from their original or best-known context and placed in a new context.

Cartesian Dualism A term which is inspired by the philosophical writings of René Descartes who argued that there is a cultural distinction drawn between the head and the body. While the head is regarded as signifying intellect and reason, the body is associated with unruly passion and excess. This dichotomy is maintained throughout most Western discourses, including art, religion and medicine.

Constructionism The opposite ideology from **essentialism** in that it argues that identification is not inherent within the person but created through interaction with culture. It is only through engagement with cultural *discourses* that people are able to identify elements such as social class, ethnicity and level of physical attractiveness.

Cyborgs A term which suggests that organic parts of the body can be replaced and enhanced by technology, hence cyborgs are human and machine. Cyborgs are often confused with robots and androids, but the key difference from the cyborg is that they are utterly artificial. The idea that any part of the body could be replaced – and enhanced – by machine components points to a time when death itself may be overcome (see **Transhumanism**).

Dichotomy At its simplest, this term means a division into two opposing groups. For example: conservative and labour, mind and body, Eastern and Western, capitalism and communism, and masculine and feminine. Nevertheless, although such binaries help us to comprehend the world, things are invariably far more dynamic, complex and chaotic than such binaries suggest.

Disability A term which describes the **identification** a subject makes because of having a specific **impairment**. While **impairment** describes the physical limitations of a specific body part, disability is the result of society's response to the subject's **impairment**.

Disability studies An area of interdisciplinary scholarship, crossing the arts, humanities and social sciences, which investigates the socio-cultural and economic politics of the identification "disabled".

Discourse A term which has two main meanings within contemporary cultural studies. First, a discourse can simply refer to any form of communication such as a literary discourse or media discourse. Second, there is the Foucauldian concept of discourse which describes cultural systems of meaning through which identifications are constructed. For example, social class is a discourse in which subjects identify as working, middle or upper (see **constructionism** and **identification**).

Embodiment A term used in different ways by different writers and theorists. However, as employed in the context of this book, the term describes how the subject experiences the world through the body. We do not think of our bodies in an abstract sense but as something experienced. For example, how does it feel to sit in this particular chair or type on this specific computer keyboard? In other words, our sense of self, and its place within the world, is experienced tacitly through the body.

Enfreakment A term coined by the art critic David Hevey which describes the process in which an unusual or non-normative body is represented and exhibited as a **"freak"**.

Ergogenics Ergogenics refers to various methods, both legal and illegal, to enhance athletic performance. These range from nutritional supplements to substances such as steroids and growth hormone. The term also includes other areas that can provide a competitive advantage; for example: training equipment and psychological support.

Essentialism The opposite of **constructionism** in that it argues that identity is inherent within the subject and not a process of **identification** through social and cultural discourses.

Fetishisation A fetish is anything that stands in for something else. A religious fetish is, therefore, any icon (sign) which stands in for God/gods. Most famously, however, the term fetish was deployed within psychoanalysis (notably the writings of Sigmund Freud) in which the fetishist focuses upon a phallic object which can stand in for and disavow the lack of a penis in the loved one and therefore allay castration anxiety. More recently, the term fetishisation is used simply to describe an erotic investment in a particular part of the body. For example, a muscle fetishist may be aroused by gym-sculpted muscles. Sometimes fetishists will maintain that the fetish is the only thing which can promote erotic arousal.

"Freak" An unusual or different body which has been subject to strategies of **enfreakment** and has been represented as a "freak". The identification of "freak" exists only within discourses of representation. The body may well be different, unusual or strange but it is the strategy of representation which renders the body a "freak".

"Freak" show An archaic entertainment spectacle in which unusual bodies were exhibited to the general public for the effects of amusement, titillation and/or horror.

Gaze A term that has a variety of meanings within film, media and cultural studies. First, there is the cinematic gaze which describes the mechanism of gazing at the film text. This gaze has a masculine, heterosexual bias and was brought to the attention of film studies by the theorist Laura Mulvey, drawing upon the writings of Lacan and Freud. Second, there is the gaze of identification described in the philosophical writings of Jean Paul Sartre who argued that a person's subjectivity is only reified by being objectified (recognised) in the eyes of an other. Third, there is the disciplinary gaze associated with prison systems such as the panopticon and most famously addressed by the philosopher Michel Foucault. The panopticon prison system was the ideal disciplinary system as the inmates internalised the warden's gaze and became their own overseer. This gaze is used as a metaphor for the power and control (especially in relation to **body image**) that is exercised in contemporary, mediated culture.

Gender Gender refers to masculinity or femininity while sex refers to man and woman. In this respect, while sex is grounded in chromosomal, anatomical laws of nature, gender refers to the way in which men and women express or act their masculinity or femininity. As such, gender is culturally and contextually mutable. For example, what was deemed appropriate acts of masculinity in previous centuries may not be deemed acceptable in contemporary culture.

Gerontophobia The fear of aged people and of ageing itself. Arguably, the power of this phobia lies in the fact that old age is something that everyone will – eventually – experience.

Golden ratio Also known as "divine proportion", it is a number – 1.618 – whose ratio signifies aesthetic perfection. Wherever the golden ratio is to be found (be that in a building, a painting, a sculpture – even a person's smile), it is suggested that there is beauty. The golden ratio has been pursued by many artists, most notably Leonardo de Vinci, and also by influential architects, such as Le Corbusier.

Grotesque body A term made famous by the writer Mikhail Bakhtin. The grotesque body is set in opposition to the classical or **ideal body** and is unrefined, disproportionate and excessive. The power of the grotesque body is that it can challenge the received ideas of propriety and appropriateness. In this respect, many critics argue that the grotesque body is always a political body.

Hegemony An indirect form of government in which the ruling parties control via a form of consent as opposed to physical coercion or force. In sociology/cultural studies, critics refer to **cultural hegemony** in which ideologies and preferences are accepted as **normal** by the general public. Implicit in maintaining hegemony are media representations which show hegemonic ideas of gender, sexuality, class and **body image**.

Hyperreality A term made famous by the philosopher Jean Baudrillard which describes how contemporary culture is now saturated with mediated images so that representation may, at times, seem more real than the actual event.

Iconography Literally – "sign writing". A term which describes the arrangement of visual elements in a text. Text, in this respect, is used in the broadest sense and may refer to a visual text (painting, film) or any form of representation including a person's body. A bodybuilder's iconography, in this respect, refers to the representation of the muscled self on the competition stage.

Ideal body Although there have always been representations of the ideal body in painting and statuary, the concept of the ideal as something *attainable* for humans was not considered until the mid ninteenth century when there was an ever-increasing need to account for people in terms of workforce statistics. By formulating an idea of the average man, based on his physical characteristics and potential contribution to the workforce, the idea of the required or well-managed body came into existence. As a result, the **normal** became linked to the ideal.

Identity/Identification The term identity suggests a fixed identity (for example, class, sexuality) which does not change according to culture or context and, as such, is grounded in theories of **essentialism**. Identification, by contrast, argues that the subject is identified through the cultural systems of meaning (**discourses**) which exist in a particular culture and, as such, is underpinned by **constructionist** thinking. For example, a person stranded in isolation on a desert island would have no idea if he/she were middle class, good looking, tall, etc. It is only through engagement with cultural regimes that identifications are possible.

Impairment A term which describes the physical shortcoming of a particular body part. The Union of the Physically Impaired Against Segregation (UPIAS) outlines impairment as 'lacking part or all of a limb, or having a defective limb, organism or mechanism of the body' (1976: 3–4).

Metrosexuality An ambiguous and contentious term which, despite differing interpretations, has become very popular in recent years. It describes a metropolitan, heterosexually identified male who has the time, and economic resources, to engage in (excessive) grooming practices. A metropolitan male, arguably, devotes a considerable amount of his leisure time to shopping, going to the gym and various processes of beautification/care of self. Arguably, metrosexuality is a sympathetic response to the articulation of gay culture in metropolitan areas in which heterosexual men have emulated paradigms and practices normally associated with gay men. In most recent times, metrosexual has become a shorthand for anything (often an item of clothing) that is deemed stylish.

"Monster" The word "monster" derives from the Latin verbs *monstrare* (to show) or *monere* (to warn). "Monsters" have always existed in legends/myths/stories and have been read as warnings of divine intervention – either as omens of the wrath of God/gods or as punishment from God/gods. "Monsters" are usually identified as unsightly or ugly. Disability scholars have speculated that a number of "monsters", identified in myths and legends, may well have been inspired by sightings of non-normative (**disabled**) bodies.

Nanotechnology A term used to describe engineering at a molecular or atomic level. Although this technology is still in its infancy, the aim is to control and manipulate atoms and molecules. The term also refers to the development of small machines that can be injected into the body to, for example, destroy cancerous cells or clean the arteries.

Non-human A term that suggests a creature or object that has certain human characteristics, but insufficient enough to be labelled as human.

Normal A term used to describe something which is requisite for the subject – often on a biological level. For example, it is normal that the human heart beat in a certain way or else the subject will become unwell.

Normative A term which refers to something which is culturally ascribed as **normal** but without any biological foundation. For example, in Anglo-American culture it is normative to eat lunch at 1.00 pm rather than **normal**.

Panopticon The "ideal" prison system in which an amphitheatre of cells surrounds a central warden's tower. The prison inmates learn that they are subject to surveillance from the central warden's tower and, over time, internalise this **gaze** so that they become their own overseers. This panoptic prison system is used as metaphor to describe the disciplining **gaze** of contemporary culture.

Patriarchy The term for a social system in which masculinity is dominant and males hold leading roles in social and cultural organisation. The opposite is a matriarchal culture.

Performance A term which describes playing or acting a specific role. The subject is on the stage performing the role of King Lear. Performance is a voluntary effect which the subject can shape or alter and should not be confused with **performative**.

Performative Often used incorrectly as a synonym for **performance**. However, **performance** is voluntary while performativity is not. The term comes from the linguist John Austin who divided language into two categories: constative and performative. Constative language merely describes what is happening. Performative language changes the situation. The most common example of a performative utterance is the marriage ceremony in which the priest or vicar pronounces two people to be married. The priest's performative utterance has now changed the status of the two people in the church. This critical concept of performativity was most famously reworked by Judith Butler who argued that gender is a performative effect. In other words, our gender is created by particular acts and gestures which performatively construct **identifications** of masculinity or femininity.

Politics of pity A term coined by the political theorist Hannah Arendt. The politics of pity functions in two main ways: first, it foregrounds the spectacle of suffering making it into something to be observed. Second, it maintains a distinction between those who suffer and those who observe them. For example, parents are not implicated in a politics of pity if their child is suffering but they are when they watch a mediated representation of a body they don't know.

Postfeminism A *highly* contentious term which has been the subject of considerable debate within gender studies over the past decade. First, postfeminism can be read as a simple backlash against the achievements of second wave feminism. In this reading, a postfeminist is actively dismissing the politics of feminism in a wish to return to prefeminism. Second, postfeminism can be read as a belief that feminist struggle is over; equality has been achieved and therefore feminist politics are no longer required. Third, postfeminism can be read as the postfeminist acknowledging the achievements of feminism and articulating a "softer" form of feminism in which *political* struggle is no longer deemed appropriate. Fourth, postfeminism can be read as representative of postmodern culture's embrace of irony in which the postfeminist may only be "toying" or "playing" with elements of a prefeminist identification because she is located in a "knowing" culture in which everyone understands the "irony". This relates to the final point (on which all critics agree) that a postfeminist identification is the privilege of middle-class, well-to-do women who are fortunate enough to be located in a sophisticated, educated culture.

Resistance A complex term and one particularly embraced by Michel Foucault in his writings on power. Throughout history there have been many types of resistance. On an obvious level there is the active resistance which takes place between two warring factions with one side resisting the attack of the other. Similarly, workers may resist a pay cut through striking. However, there is also resistance which takes place at the level of cultural negotiation and can be demonstrated through **iconography** or **discourse**. As such, resistance may occur on many levels: it may be overtly political, and demonstrated through street marches and the affirmation of a quantifiable presence, or it may be a much more moderate display. For example, a school child may be resisting the powers of the school by dying his/her hair a lurid colour. It is interesting to note that whenever resistance first occurs it is often demonstrated through the body's **iconography**.

Situationism Originating in France in 1957, the Situationists (or Situationist International) were a political and artistic movement. One of their primary concerns was with the way that capitalism has made people's lives deeply inauthentic, banal and passive. A key figure of this movement was Guy Debord (1931–1994) who published his book *The Society of the Spectacle* in 1967 which provides a strong attack on a modern society where "being" has slipped into "having" and people are increasingly defined by what they purchase. Debord suggests that human relationships have become increasingly mediated through images; indeed for him, the image is now more important than physical things. Such thinking has been extremely influential on postmodern thought and, in particular, the work of Jean Baudrillard (see **hyperreality**).

Size zero A woman's clothing size in the US catalogue of clothing sizes. However, the term is more often used in contemporary Western culture to signify an extremely thin body which aspires to the proportions of catwalk models.

Stereotype A representation of a specific group of people which simplifies the group by reducing them to one feature. Stereotypes are not always negative ("the French are good cooks") but they are implicit in discourses of power in which the dominant group represent a minority or "other" in a simplified, reductive fashion.

Subculture A group of people within a culture who differentiate themselves from the dominant culture in which they are located. This difference is often articulated at the level of style or **iconography** although it may also be at the level of linguistic **discourse**. Members of the subcultural group will recognise other members through a reading of the **iconography** or **discourse**.

Symbiotic relationship This term refers to the way that two organisms can profit from each other. For example, there is a symbiotic relationship between people and their domestic pets such as a dog or cat. Both human and pet have benefits from this relationship. Hence, a dog gives affection to its owner and offers companionship; in return, the dog is given love, food and shelter.

Technocopia Although no such word is listed in the dictionary, for us, technocopia is used to suggest, like the term cornucopia, an abundance of something: in this case, technology.

Transgression A term which describes the act of a subject violating and/or crossing rules or boundaries. For example, if a male body performs femininity he is committing an act of **gender** transgression. However, it is important to remember that transgression always affirms an acknowledgement (and, arguably, a respect) for that boundary. Transgression also can only have a limited effect as the subject has crossed one set of boundaries only to situate him/herself within another (sub)culture in which another series of rules and regulations are to be found.

Transhumanism An intellectual and cultural movement that views technology as radically lengthening human life expectancy through scientific developments such as genetic engineering, cloning and nanotechnology. Transhumanists also show great interest in technologies that offer other possibilities such as increased intelligence that moves humans far beyond their own biological limits (hence the term transhuman).

BIBLIOGRAPHY

Adams, Rachel (2001) *Sideshow USA: Freaks and the American Cultural Imagination* (Chicago: University of Chicago Press)

Allen, Dennis (2006) 'Making Over Masculinity: A Queer "I" for the Straight Guy', Genders.org 44, http://genders.org/g44/g44_allen.html, accessed 21 May 2013

Almaguer, Tomas (1991) 'Chicano Men: A Cartography of Homosexual Identity and Behaviour', *differences: A Journal of Feminist Cultural Studies*, 3(2): 75–100

Andrews, Maggie (2003) 'Calendar Ladies: Popular Culture, Sexuality and the Middle-Class, Middle-Aged Domestic Woman', *Sexualities*, 6(3–4): 385–403

Anthes, Emily (2013) 'The race to create "insect cyborgs"', *The Observer*, 17 February, http://www.theguardian.com/science/2013/feb/17/race-to-create-insect-cyborgs, accessed 2 February 2014

Asimov, Isaac (1987) 'Cybernetic Organism', http://www.e-reading.mobi/chapter.php/81944/2/Wu_-_Cyborg.html, accessed 6 January 2013

Attwood, Feona (ed.) (2009) *Mainstreaming Sex: The Sexualization of Western Culture* (London: I. B.Tauris)

Baggott, Jim (2005) *A Beginner's Guide to Reality* (London: Penguin)

Bakhtin, Mikhail (1984) *Rabelais and His World* (trans. H. Iswolsky) (Bloomington, IN: Indiana University Press)

Balsamo, Anne Marie (1999) *Technologies of the Gendered Body: Reading Cyborg Women* (Durham, NC: Duke University Press) Barnes, Colin and Mercer, Geoff (2003) *Disability* (Cambridge: Polity Press)

Bartky, Sandra Lee (1990) *Femininity and Domination: Studies in the Phenomenology of Oppression* (London: Routledge)

Baudrillard, Jean (1983) *Simulations* (New York: Semiotext(e))

Bell, David (2001) *An Introduction to Cybercultures* (London: Routledge)

Bell, David and Kennedy, Barbara M. (2002) *The Cybercultures Reader* (New York: Routledge)

Berger, John (1975) *Ways of Seeing* (Middlesex: Penguin Books Ltd)

Berila, Beth and Choudhuri, Devika Dibya (2005) 'Metrosexuality the Middle Class Way: Exploring Race, Class and Gender', in *Queer Eye for the Straight Guy*, Genders.org 42, http://www.genders.org/g42_berila_choudhuri.html, accessed 21 May 2013

Best, Steven and Kellner, Douglas (1997) *The Postmodern Turn* (New York and London: Guildford Press)

Blaikie, Andrew (1997) 'Beside the Sea: Visual Imagery, Ageing and Heritage', *Ageing and Society*, 17: 629–648

Bogdan, Robert (1988) *Freak Show: Presenting Human Oddities for Amusement and Profit* (Chicago: University of Chicago Press)

Bordo, Susan (1993) *Unbearable Weight: Feminism, Western Culture, and the Body* (Berkeley, CA: University of California Press)

——(1999) *The Male Body: A New Look at Men in Public and in Private* (New York: Farrar, Straus and Giroux)

Boynton, Victoria and Malin, Jo (ed.) (2005) *Encyclopedia of Women's Autobiography: A–J* (Portsmouth, NH: Greenwood Press)

Branston, Gill and Stafford, Roy (2003) *The Media Student's Book*, 3rd edition (London and New York: Routledge)

Bukatman, Scott (1993) *Terminal Identity: The Virtual Subject in Postmodern Science Fiction* (Durham, NC: Duke University Press)

——(1997) *Blade Runner* (London: BFI)

Butler, Judith (1990) *Gender Trouble: Feminism and the Subversion of Identity* (London and New York: Routledge)

——(1993) *Bodies That Matter: On the Discursive Limits of Sex* (London: Routledge)

Cahill, Susan (2010) 'Through the Looking Glass: Fairy-Tale Cinema and the Spectacle of Femininity in *Stardust* and *The Brothers Grimm*', *Marvels & Tales*, 24(1): 57–67

Caplan, Jane (ed.) (2000) *Written on the Body: The Tattoo in European and American History* (London: Reaktion Books)

Case, Amber (2010) 'We are all cyborgs now', presentation at TED, http://www.ted.com/talks/amber_case_we_are_all_cyborgs_now.html, accessed 2 February 2013

Chapman, James (2006) *Inside the Tardis: The Worlds of Doctor Who* (London and New York: I. B. Tauris)

Chivers, Sally (2006) 'Baby Jane Grew Up: The Dramatic Intersection of Age with Disability', *Canadian Review of American Studies*, 36(2): 211–227

——(2011) *The Silvering Screen: Old Age and Disability in Cinema* (Toronto: University of Toronto Press)

Church of Body Modification website at http://uscobm.com, accessed 12 October 2013

Clark, Andy (2003) *Natural-Born Cyborgs: Minds, Technologies, and the Future of Human Intelligence* (Oxford: Oxford University Press)

Clark, Kenneth (1957) *The Nude: A Study of Ideal Art* (London: John Murray)

Clynes, Manfred and Kline, Nathan (1995) 'Cyborgs in Space', in Chris Hables Gray, Heidi J. Figueroa-Sarriera and Steven Mentor (eds) *The Cyborg Handbook* (New York and London: Routledge)

Coles, Fen (1999) 'Feminist Charms and Outrageous Arms', in Janet Price and Margrit Shildrick (eds) *Feminist Theory and the Body: A Reader* (Edinburgh: Edinburgh University Press)

Copjec, Joan (1989) 'The Orthopsychic Subject: Film Theory and the Reception of Lacan', *October*, 49: 53–71

Couper, Alastair (2009) *Sailors and Traders: A Maritime History of the Pacific Peoples* (Hawaii: University of Hawaii Press)

Creed, Barbara (1992) 'Dark Desires: Male Masochism in the Horror Film', in Steve Cohan and Ina Rae Hark (eds) *Screening the Male: Exploring Masculinities in Hollywood* (London: Routledge)

Davis, Kathy (1995) *Reshaping the Female Body* (New York: Routledge)

——(2002) 'A Dubious Equality: Men, Women and Cosmetic Surgery', *Body & Society*, 8(1): 49–65

Davis, Lennard J. (1995) *Enforcing Normalcy: Disability, Deafness, and the Body* (New York: Verso)

Dawson, Mark (2012) *Gentility and the Comic Theatre of Late Stuart London* (Cambridge: Cambridge University Press)

De Beauvoir, Simone (1970) *The Coming of Age* (New York: Norton)

Delueze, Gilles and Guattari, Felix (2004) *Anti-Oedipus* (London: Continuum)

DeMello, Margo (2000) *Bodies of Inscription: A Cultural History of the Modern Tattoo Community* (Durham, NC, and London: Duke University Press)

Descartes, René (1969) *Passions of the Soul* in *Philosophical Works of Descartes* (2 vols) (trans. Elizabeth S. Haldane and G. R. T. Ross) (Cambridge: Cambridge University Press)

Dolan, Josephine and Tincknell, Estella (2012) *Ageing Femininities: Troubling Representations* (Cambridge: Cambridge Scholar Publishing)

Dominick, Richard (ed.) (1999) *Jerry Springer's Wildest Shows Ever!* (London: Little Brown)

Douglas, Susan J. (2010) *Enlightened Sexism: The Seductive Message that Feminism's Work is Done* (New York: Times Books)

Drexler, K. Eric (1996) *Engines of Creation* (London: HarperCollins)

Duniluk, Judith C. (2003) *Women's Sexuality Across the Life Span: Challenging Myths, Creating Meanings* (New York: Guilford Press)

Dutton, Kenneth R. (1995) *The Perfectible Body: The Western Ideal of Physical Perfection* (London: Cassell)

Dyer, Richard (1982) 'Don't Look Now: The Male Pin-Up', *Screen*, 23(3–4): 61–67

Epstein, Samuel (2009) *Toxic Beauty: How Cosmetics and Personal-Care Products Endanger Your Health … and What You Can Do About It* (Dallas: Benbella Books)

Farmer, Brett (2000) *Spectacular Passions: Cinema, Fantasy, Gay Male Spectatorships* (Durham, NC, and London: Duke University Press)

Favazza, Armando (2011) *Under Siege: Self-Mutilation, Non-Suicidal Self-Injury, and Body Modification in Culture and Psychiatry* (Baltimore: Johns Hopkins University Press)

Featherstone, Mike (ed.) (2000) *Body Modification* (London: Sage)

Featherstone, Mike and Burrows, Roger (1995) *Cyberspace/Cyberbodies/Cyberpunk* (London: Sage)

Featherstone, Mike and Wernick, Andrew (eds) (1995) *Images of Aging: Cultural Representations of Later Life* (London: Routledge)

Foster, Lynn Vasco (2002) *Handbook to Life in the Ancient Maya World* (Oxford and New York: Oxford University Press)

Foucault, Michel (1969) *Madness and Civilization* (London: Tavistock)

——(1977) *Discipline and Punish: The Birth of the Prison* (trans. Alan Sheridan) (Harmondsworth: Penguin)

Fraser, Nancy (1989) *Unruly Practices: Power, Discourse, and Gender in Contemporary Social Theory* (Cambridge: Polity Press)

Freeland, Cynthia (2002) 'Penetrating Keanu', in William Irwin (ed.) *The Matrix and Philosophy* (Peru, IL: Carus Publishing)

Freeman, Charles (1999) *The Greek Achievement: The Foundation of the Western World* (New York: Viking)

Fukuyama, Francis (2002) *Our Postmodern Future: Consequences of the Biotechnology Revolution* (New York: Farrar, Straus and Giroux)

Fussell, Sam (1994) 'Bodybuilder Americanus', in Laurence Goldstein (ed.) *The Male Body: Features, Destinies, Exposures* (Ann Arbor, MI: The University of Michigan Press)

Gamson, Joshua (1998) *Freaks Talk Back: Tabloid Talk Shows and Sexual Nonconformity* (Chicago: University of Chicago Press)

Garland Thomson, Rosemarie (1996) 'Introduction: From Wonder to Error – A Genealogy of Freak Discourse in Modernity', in Rosemarie Thomson (ed.) *Freakery: Cultural Spectacles of the Extraordinary Body* (New York: New York University Press)

——(1997) *Extraordinary Bodies: Figuring Physical Disability in American Culture and Literature* (New York: Columbia University Press)

——(2002) 'Integrating Disability, Transforming Feminist Theory', *NWSA Journal*, 14(3): 1–32

——(2009) *Staring: How We Look* (Oxford: Oxford University Press)

Gauntlett, David (2008) *Media, Gender and Identity: An Introduction* (London: Routledge)

Giddens, Anthony (1991) *Modernity and Self-Identity: Self and Society in the Late Modern Age* (Cambridge: Polity Press)

Gill, Rosalind (2007) *Gender and the Media* (Cambridge: Polity Press)

Gilleard, Chris and Higgs, Paul (2005) *Contexts of Ageing: Class, Cohort and Community* (Cambridge: Polity Press)

Greer, Germaine (1992) *The Change: Women, Ageing and the Menopause* (New York: Knopf)

——(2000) *The Whole Woman* (London: Anchor) Grinding website at http://grinding.be/2008/03/20/steve-haworth-modern-body-modification-pioneer/, accessed 11 August 2013

Guinness World Records 2013 (2013) (Guinness World Records)

Gullette, Margaret Morganroth (2004) *Aged by Culture* (Chicago: University of Chicago Press)

Halberstam, Judith (1995) *Skin Shows: Gothic Horror and the Technology of Monsters* (Durham, NC, and London: Duke University Press)

Hall, Stuart (1992) 'The Question of Cultural Identity', in Stuart Hall and Tony McGrew (eds) *Modernity and its Futures* (Cambridge: Polity Press)

Haraway, Donna J. (1991) *Simians, Cyborgs and Women: The Reinvention of Nature* (New York and London: Routledge)

Hassan, Ihab (1977) 'Prometheus as Performer: Toward a Posthumanist Culture?', in Michael Benamon and Charles Caramella (eds) *Performance in Postmodern Culture* (Milwaukee, WI: Center for Twentieth Century Studies, University of Wisconsin-Milwaukee)

Hebdige, Dick (1979) *Subculture: The Meaning of Style* (London: Methuen)

Hersey, George L. (1996) *The Evolution of Allure: Sexual Selection from the Medici Venus to The Incredible Hulk* (Cambridge, MA: MIT Press)

Hevey, David (1992) *The Creatures That Time Forgot: Photography and Disability Imagery* (London: Routledge)

Heyes, Cressida and Jones, Meredith (eds) (2009) *Cosmetic Surgery: A Feminist Primer* (Farnham: Ashgate)

Higson, Andrew (2003) *English Heritage, English Cinema: Costume Drama since 1980* (Oxford: Oxford University Press)

Hill, John (1999) *British Cinema in the 1980s: Issues and Themes* (Oxford: Clarendon Press)

Holmlund, Christine (1989) 'Visible Difference and Flex Appeal: The Body, Sex, Sexuality, and Race in the *Pumping Iron* Films', *Cinema Journal*, 28(4): 38–51

Hotten, Jon (2004) *Muscle: A Writer's Trip Through a Sport with No Boundaries* (London: Yellow Jersey Press)

Human Rights Watch (2012) 'Losing Humanity: The Case Against Killer Robots', http://www.hrw.org/reports/2012/11/19/losing-humanity-0, accessed 5 January 2013

Hunter, Jack (1995) *Inside Teradome: An Illustrated History of Freak Film* (London: Creation Books)

James, Edward and Mendlesohn, Farah (eds) (2003) *The Cambridge Companion to Science Fiction* (Cambridge: Cambridge University Press)

Jermyn, Deborah (ed.) (2013) *Female Celebrity and Ageing: Back in the Spotlight* (London: Routledge)

Johnson, Rebecca L. (2008) *Nanotechnology* (Minneapolis: Lerner Publishing Group)

Jones, Geoffrey (2010) *Beauty Imagined: A History of the Global Beauty Industry* (Oxford: Oxford University Press)

Jones, Julie and Pugh, Steve (2005) 'Ageing Gay Men: Lessons from the Sociology of Embodiment', *Men and Masculinities*, 7(3): 248–260

Jones, Meredith (2008) 'Makeover Culture's Dark Side: Breasts, Death and Lolo Ferrari', *Body & Society*, 14(1): 89–104

Kellner, Douglas (1995) *Media Culture: Cultural Studies, Identity and Politics between the Modern and the Postmodern* (London and New York: Routledge)

Kirkup, Gill; Janes, Linda; Woodward, Kath and Hovenden, Fiona (2000) *The Gendered Cyborg: A Reader* (London: Routledge)

Klein, Alan M. (1993) *Little Big Men: Bodybuilding Subculture and Gender Construction* (Albany, NY: State University of New York Press)

Klesse, Christian (2000) '"Modern Primitivism": Non-Mainstream Body Modification and Racialized Representation', in Mike Featherstone (ed.) *Body Modification* (London: Sage)

Koch, Christof and Crick, Francis (2001) 'The Zombie Within', *Nature*, 411: 21 June, http://codatest4.library.caltech.edu/249/1/397.pdf, accessed 10 December 2013

Krell, Farnell (ed.) (1977) *Martin Heidegger: Basic Writings* (New York: Harper and Row)

Kuhn, Annette (1997) 'The Body and Cinema: Some Problems for Feminism', in Sandra Kemp and Judith Squires (eds) *Feminisms* (Oxford: Oxford University Press)

Kuwahara, Makikio (2005) *Tattoo: An Anthropology* (New York: Berg)

Laisne, Claude (1995) *Art of Ancient Greece: Painting Sculpture Architecture* (Paris: Terrail)

Lane, Richard (2000) *Jean Baudrillard* (London and New York: Routledge)

Lee, Khoon Choy (2000) *Pioneers of Modern China: Understanding the Inscrutable Chinese* (Singapore: World Scientific Publishing)

Locks, Adam and Richardson, Niall (eds) (2011) *Critical Readings in Bodybuilding* (London: Routledge)

Luckhurst, Roger (2005) *Science Fiction* (Cambridge: Polity Press)

Lyotard, Jean-François (1984) *The Postmodern Condition: A Report on Knowledge* (Manchester: Manchester University Press)

Maki (2009) 'Body Inflation', in *Bizarre* magazine, at http://www.bizarremag.com/tattoos-and-bodyart/body-mods/7801/body_inflation.html, accessed 14 September 2013

Marcus, Griel (2001) *Lipstick Traces: A Secret History of the Twentieth Century* (London: Faber and Faber)

Marks, Deborah (1999) *Disability: Controversial Debates and Psycho-Social Perspectives* (London: Routledge)

Mason, Fran (1999) 'Loving the Technological Undead: Cyborg Sex and Necrophilia in Richard Calder's *Dead* Trilogy', in Michele Aaron (ed.) *The Body's Perilous Pleasures: Dangerous Desires and Contemporary Cultures* (Edinburgh: Edinburgh University Press)

McCaffery, Larry (1994) *Storming the Reality Studio: A Casebook of Cyberpunk and Postmodern Science Fiction* (London: Duke University Press)

McGruer, Robert (2006) *Crip Theory: Cultural Signs of Queerness and Disability* (New York: New York University Press)

McLuhan, Marshall (1994) *Understanding Media: The Extensions of Man* (London: MIT Press)

McNair, Brian (2002) *Striptease Culture: Sex, Media and the Democratization of Desire* (London: Routledge)

McRobbie, Angela (1997) 'Postfeminism and Popular Culture: Bridget Jones and the New Gender Regime', in Tasker, Yvonne and Negra, Diane (eds) *Interrogating Postfeminism: Gender and the Politics of Popular Culture* (Durham, NC: Duke University Press)

——(2009) *The Aftermath of Feminism* (London: Sage)

Medhurst, Andy (1997) 'Camp', in Andy Medhurst and Sally Munt (eds) *Lesbian and Gay Studies: A Critical Introduction* (London: Cassell)

Mercer, John (2012) 'Coming of Age: Problematising Gay Porn and the Eroticised Older Man', *Journal of Gender Studies*, 21(3): 313–326

Merleau-Ponty, Maurice (1976) *The Primacy of Perception: And Other Essays on Phenomenological Psychology, the Philosophy of Art, History and Politics* (Evanston, IL: Northwestern University Press)

——(1981) *The Phenomenology of Perception* (London: Routledge)

Miller, Toby (2005) 'A Metrosexual Eye on *Queer Guy*', *GLQ*, 11(1): 112–117

Monaghan, Lee F. (2001) *Bodybuilding, Drugs and Risk* (London: Routledge)

——(2008) *Men and the War on Obesity: A Sociological Study* (London: Routledge)

Monaghan, Lee F. and Atkinson, Michael (2014, forthcoming) Challenging Masculinity Myths: Understanding Physical Cultures (Farnham: Ashgate)

Monaghan, Lee F.; Colls, R. and Evans, B. (eds) (2014, forthcoming) *Obesity Discourse and Fat Politics: Research, Critique and Interventions* (London: Routledge)

Moravec, Hans (1988) *Mind Children: The Future of Robot and Human Intelligence* (Cambridge, MA: Harvard University Press)

Morey, Anne (2011) 'Grotesquerie as Marker of Success in Aging Female Stars', in Su Holmes and Diane Negra (eds) *In the Limelight and Under the Microscope: Forms and Functions of Female Celebrity* (New York: Continuum)

Moseley, Rachel (2009) 'A Landscape of Desire: Cornwall as Romantic Setting in *Love Story* and *Ladies in Lavender*', in Melanie Bell and Melanie Williams (eds) *British Women's Cinema* (London: Routledge)

Nead, Lynda (1992) *The Female Nude: Art, Obscenity and Sexuality* (London: Routledge)

Negra, Diane (2009) *What a Girl Wants? Fantasizing the Reclamation of Self in Postfeminism* (London: Routledge)

Negrin, Llewellyn (2002) 'Cosmetic Surgery and the Eclipse of Identity', *Body & Society*, 8: (4): 21–42

Nelson, Jack (1994) 'Broken Images: Portrayals of Those with disabilities in the American Media', in J. Nelson (ed.) *People with Disabilities, the Media and the Information Age* (Westport, CT: Greenwood Press)

Norden, Martin F. (1994) *The Cinema of Isolation: A History of Physical Disability in the Movies* (New Brunswick, NJ: Rutgers University Press)

O'Brien, Daniel (2000) *SF/UK: How British Science Fiction Changed the World* (London: Reynolds and Hearn)

Orbach, Susie (2009) *Bodies* (London: Profile)

Palmer, Gareth (ed.) (2008) *Exposing Lifestyle Television: The Big Reveal* (Farnham: Ashgate)

Paré, Ambroise (1982) *On Monsters and Marvels* (trans. Janis L. Pallister) (Chicago: University of Chicago Press)

Pitts, Victoria (2003) *In the Flesh: The Cultural Politics of Body Modification* (New York: Palgrave Macmillan)

Plante, Lori G. (2007) *Bleeding to Ease the Pain: Cutting, Self-Injury, and the Adolescent Search for Self* (Portland, OR: Praeger)

Polhemus, Ted and Marenko, Betti (2004) *Hot Bodies, Cool Styles: New Techniques in Self Adornment* (London: Thames and Hudson)

Pope, Harrison; Phillips, Kate and Olivardia, Roberto (2000) *The Adonis Complex: The Secret Crisis of Male Body Obsession* (New York and London: Simon and Schuster)

Randall, Housk (2002) *Piercing: A Modern Anthology* (London: Salmander)

Rexbeye, Helle and Povlsen, Jørgen (2007) 'Visual Signs of Ageing: What Are We Looking at?', *International Journal of Ageing and Later Life*, 2(10): 61–83

Rich, E.; Monaghan, Lee F. and Aphramor, L. (eds) (2011) *Debating Obesity: Critical Perspectives* (London: Palgrave Macmillan)

Richardson, Niall (2004) 'The Queer Activity of Extreme Male Bodybuilding: Gender Dissidence, Auto Eroticism and Hysteria', *Social Semiotics*, 14(1): 49–65

——(2008) 'Flex Rated! Female Bodybuilding: Feminist Resistance or Erotic Spectacle?', *Journal of Gender Studies*, 17(4): 289–301

——(2009) *The Queer Cinema of Derek Jarman: Critical and Cultural Readings* (London: I. B. Tauris)

——(2010) *Transgressive Bodies: Representations in Film and Popular Culture* (Farnham: Ashgate)

——(2011) 'Strategies of Enfreakment: Representations of Contemporary Bodybuilding' in Adam Locks and Niall Richardson (eds) *Critical Readings in Bodybuilding* (London: Routledge)

——(forthcoming) *Ageing Femininity: Representations of Older Women in Cinema* (London: I. B. Tauris)

Richardson, Niall and Wearing, Sadie (2014) *Key Concerns in Media Studies: Gender and Media* (London: Palgrave Macmillan)

Richardson, Niall; Smith, Clarissa and Werndly, Angela (2013) *Studying Sexualities: Theories, Representations, Practices* (London: Palgrave Macmillan)

Roberts, Adam (2006) *Science Fiction* (London and New York: Routledge)

Robinson, Dave (1999) *Nietzsche and Postmodernism* (Cambridge: Icon Books)

Romano, John (1996) 'Drugs Versus Natural: The Future of Bodybuilding – Women on Steroids', *Muscular Development*, March: 131, 172, 186

Rowe, John and Kahn, Robert (1997) 'Successful Aging', *The Gerontologist*, 37(4): 433–440

Saint-Hilaire, Étienne Geoffroy (1822) *Philosophie Anatomique: Des Monstruités Humaines, Ouvrage Contenant une Classification des Monsters* (Oxford: Oxford University Press)

Sandberg, Linn (2008) 'The Old, the Ugly and the Queer: Thinking Old Age in Relation to Queer Theory', *Graduate Journal of Social Science*, 5(2): 117–139

Sarup, Madan (1996) *Identity, Culture and the Postmodern World* (Edinburgh: Edinburgh University Press)

Schulze, Laurie (1990) 'On the Muscle', in Jane Gaines and Charlotte Herzog (eds) *Fabrications* (London: Routledge)

Scott, Linda M. (2005) *Fresh Lipstick: Redressing Fashion and Feminism* (New York: Palgrave Macmillan)

Seymour, Sabine (2010) *Fashionable Technology: The Intersection of Design, Fashion, Science, and Technology* (New York: Springer)

Shakespeare, Tom (1992) 'A Response to Liz Crow', *Coalition*, September: 40–42

Shapiro, Eve (2010) *Gender Circuits: Bodies and Identities in a Technological Age* (New York: Routledge)

Shildrick, Margrit (2002) *Embodying the Monster: Encounters with the Vulnerable Self* (London: Sage)

Shilling, Chris (2003) *The Body and Social Theory* (London: Sage)

Shingler, Martin (1995) 'Masquerade or Drag? Bette Davis and the Ambiguities of Gender', *Screen*, 36(3): 179–192

Shippert, Claudia (2007) 'Can Muscles be Queer? Reconsidering the Transgressive Hyper-Built Body', *Journal of Gender Studies*, 16(2): 155–171

Silver, Catherine B. (2003) 'Gendered Identities in Old Age: Toward (De)gendering?', *Journal of Aging Studies*, 17: 379–397

Simpson, Mark (1992) *Male Impersonators* (London: Cassell)

Skeggs, Beverly (1997) *Formations of Class and Gender: Becoming Respectable* (London: Sage)

——(2003) *Class, Self, Culture* (London: Routledge)

Sleight, Graham (2012) *The Doctor's Monsters: Meanings of the Monstrous in Doctor Who* (London and New York: I. B. Tauris)

Spelman, Elizabeth (1982) 'Woman as Body: Ancient and Contemporary Views', *Feminist Studies*, 8(1): 108–131

Spinks, Jennifer (2005) 'Wondrous Monsters: Representing Conjoined Twins in Early Sixteenth Century German Broadsheets', *Parergon*, 22(2): 77–112

Sriraman, Bharath; Freiman, Viktor and Lirette-Pitre, Nicole (ed) (2009) *Interdisciplinarity, Creativity, and Learning: Mathematics with Literature* (North Carolina: Information Age Publishing)

Stephens, Elizabeth (2006) 'Cultural Fictions of the Freak Body: Coney Island and the Postmodern Sideshow', *Continuum: Journal of Media and Cultural Studies*, 20(4): 485–98

Stoddard, Karen M. (1983) *Saints and Shrews: Women and Aging in American Popular Culture* (London: Greenwood Press)

Storr, Marl (2003) *Latex and Lingerie: Shopping for Pleasure at Ann Summers* (Oxford and New York: Berg)

Sweet, Matthew (2001) *Inventing the Victorians* (London: Faber and Faber)

Tasker, Yvonne and Negra, Diane (eds) (2007) *Interrogating Postfeminism: Gender and the Politics of Popular Culture* (Durham, NC: Duke University Press)

Telegraph online (2010) 'Computer gamers have reactions of pilots but bodies of chain smokers', http://www.telegraph.co.uk/technology/video-games/7808860/Computer-gamers-have-reactions-of-pilots-but-bodies-of-chain-smokers.html, accessed 10 February 2013

Torres, Sandra and Hammarström, Gunhild (2006) 'To age well is not to age at all: elderly peoples' notions of successful aging', paper presented at the 59th Annual Scientific Meeting of The Gerontological Society of America, Nov 16–20, Dallas, Texas

UPIAS (1976) 'Fundamental Principles of Disability' (London: Union of the Physically Impaired Against Segregation)

Vale, V. and Juno, Andrea (1989) *Modern Primitives: An Investigation of Contemporary Adornment and Ritual* (New York: Re/Search Publications)

Varadan, Vijay K.; Pillai, A. Sivathanu; Mukherji, Debashish; Dwivedi, Mayank and Chen, Linfeng (2010) *Nanoscience and Nanotechnology in Engineering* (Singapore: World Scientific Publishing)

Varies, Tina (2009) 'Reading the Sexie Oldie: Gender, Age(ing) and Embodiment', *Sexualities*, 12(4): 503–524

Wahl, Otto (1995) *Media Madness: Public Images of Mental Illness* (New Brunswick, NJ: Rutgers University Press)

Walter, Natasha (2010) *Living Dolls: The Return of Sexism* (London: Virago)

Warrick, Patricia S. (1980) *The Cybernetic Imagination in Science Fiction* (Cambridge, MA: MIT)

Wearing, Sadie (2007) 'Subjects of Rejuvenation: Ageing in Postfeminist Culture and Feminist Critique', in Yvonne Takser and Diane Negra (eds) *Interrogating Postfeminism: Gender and the Politics of Popular Culture* (Durham, NC: Duke University Press)

——(2009) 'The New Mrs Robinsons? Transgenerational Sexual Configurations in Contemporary Cinema', in Rosalind Gill and Christina Scharff (eds) *New Femininities: Postfeminism, Neoliberalism and Identity* (London: Palgrave Macmillan)

Weibel, Kathryn (1977) *Mirror, Mirror: Images of Women Reflected in Popular Culture* (New York: Anchor Press)

Wells, H. G. (2008) *The War of the Worlds* (Rockville, MD: Phoenix Pick)

Wells, H. G., with contributions by Panshin, Alexi; Panshin, Cory and Cook, Paul (2009) *The Time Machine* (Rockville, MD: Phoenix Pick)

Whelehan, Imelda (2009) 'Not to Be Looked at: Older Women in Recent British Cinema', in Melanie Bell and Melanie Williams (eds) *British Women's Cinema* (London: Routledge)

White, Philip G.; Young, Kevin and McTeer, William G. (1995) 'Sport, Masculinity and the Injured Body', in Donald Sabo and David Frederick Gordon (eds) *Men's Health and Illness: Gender, Power and the Body* (London: Sage)

Wilson, Elizabeth (1993) 'Is Transgression Transgressive?', in Joseph Bristow and Anglia R. Wilson (eds) *Activating Theory: Lesbian, Gay, Bisexual Politics* (London: Lawrence & Wishart)

Winge, Theresa M. (2012) *Body Style* (London: Berg)

Wolf, Naomi (1991) *The Beauty Myth: How Images of Beauty Are Used Against Women* (London: Vintage)

Yates, Alayne (1991) *Compulsive Exercise and the Eating Disorders: Toward an Integrated Theory of Activity* (New York: Brunner/Mazel)

Yates, Dorian (1995) 'On a Wing and a Prayer', *Flex*, February: 27–33

Zalcock, Bev (1998) *Renegade Sisters: Girl Gangs on Film* (London: Creation Books)

Zola, Irving (1985) 'Depictions of Disability – Metaphor, Message and Medium in the Media: A Research and Political Agenda', *Social Science Journal*, 22(4): 5–17

INDEX

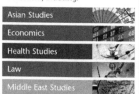